CONTENTS

Introduction 9

1935	11
1936	57
1937	95
1938	133
1939	175
1940s	187
1950s	239

LOCH NESS:
Back Into The Depths

More Original Newspaper Accounts Of the Loch Ness Monster 1935-1955

Edited & Compiled by
PATRICK J GALLAGHER

Copyright © 2016 Patrick J Gallagher
All rights reserved.
ISBN: 153095679X
ISBN-13: 978-1530956791

This one is for Natalie, my wonderful and inspirational friend. Here's to your favourite not-so-scary monster.

INTRODUCTION

The 1930s were most definitely the boom years for the Loch Ness Monster, that enigmatic cryptid which supposedly dwells in one of Scotland's deepest lakes.

The imagination of the world was excited by the apparent emergence of the creature in 1933, with dozens of sightings reported by people from all walks of life. The high volume of sightings continued through 1934, making these two years the all-time peak in "Nessie" sightings.

But then, gradually, the number of reported sightings in the press began to taper off. Never again would "Nessie Fever" grip the Scottish Highlands in quite the same way. There were occasional spikes in reports, but nothing to match those original two years.

That decline is reflected in this volume, which contains original newspaper accounts pertaining to the Loch Ness Monster between 1935 and 1955.

My previous book on the subject, "Loch Ness: From Out Of The Depths," only covered the years 1933-34, but ran to a fairly hefty 380 pages. This book, which covers the following 20 years (1935-55) comes in at only 260 pages, with the bulk of those detailing reports from the remaining years of the 1930s.

Probably one of the main contributing factors to the reduction in sightings is the Second World War. During those years in the 1940s as the war raged in Europe and beyond, there were fewer eyes on the loch as the annual tourist trade which accounted for a number of monster sightings, came to a virtual standstill.

This is borne out by the rise in sightings in 1947, as life returned to normal in post-war Scotland, and tourists once again flocked to Loch Ness, increasing the chances of spotting the creature that still seemed to lurk in its depths.

Another reason for the decline in reports may simply be that public interest in the monster, or at least the level of interest perceived by the newspapers, had begun to wane. Nessie sightings had become almost mundane in a lot of cases, rating only a few sentences for each report compared to the column inches previously devoted to the subject.

It wasn't until the late 50s-early 60s, with the rise of television media and more sophisticated means of "monster hunting" that the Loch Ness Monster once again reasserted itself as a strong force in the public consciousness, making Nessie even more of a world-wide celebrity than before.

Theories abound, and there is still no definitive proof or answer to the mystery of Loch Ness. But perhaps that's okay. The mystery, the legend, of "Nessie" fires our imaginations, makes us consider the as-yet undiscovered "could be's" in the world, and inspires some souls to explore and uncover more about our world than was previously known.

And that can only be a good thing.

1935

Aberdeen Journal - Tuesday 15 January 1935

LOCH NESS MONSTER RE-APPEARS.
Of Huge Dimensions With Barrel-Like Humps.

The Loch Ness monster was seen in Glenurquhart Bay early yesterday by Mr Duncan Fraser, a ploughman employed by Mr Alexander Ross, Glenurquhart.

Mr Fraser told a "Press and Journal" correspondent that he had watched a large beast, showing several humps like barrels, for five minutes - although no head or tail was seen. Witness stated that from the great splashing it caused, he judged the creature to be of huge dimensions.

While under observation, witness added, the beast moved with a quick up-and-down motion, diving and re-appearing several times before it finally submerged towards the Inverness end of the Loch.

Sunday Post - Sunday 20 January 1935

'NESSIE' WATCHED FOR HALF AN HOUR
Humps as Big as Beehives
MONKS THRILLED AT FORT-AUGUSTUS

Two Benedictine Fathers, several lay brothers, and three boys of the Abbey schools, Fort-Augustus, had a rare thrill about noon yesterday, when they watched from the grounds of St Benedict's Abbey the Loch Ness monster disport itself at the west end of the loch for over half an hour.

In an interview Father O'Connell said he watched the monster through an admiralty telescope which is guaranteed up to ten miles.

It first appeared off the Inchnacardoch side of the loch, crossed slowly towards the opposite shore a mile away, turned east in the direction of the Horseshoe, and then came towards Fort-Augustus.

Three humps were in view, each about a foot high.

He thought its speed was about six miles an hour.

Father Sole said frankly he had been quite sceptical regarding the existence of the monster or strange creature in Loch Ness. And, like Father O'Connell, put the so-called appearance down to rowing boats, motor boats, or even ducks flitting about the surface when the light was uncertain.

The living creature he had just seen, however, proved that the loch does harbour a strange animal, which is neither a seal nor otter.

At times, he continued, the object showed three humps, which would suddenly merge into two, and then again only one long black object would be seen. Each hump, he had no hesitation in saying, was 10 to 12 feet distant from its neighbour, and, as all were certainly joined together, the total length was 30 feet or more.

No head or tail was seen, and, to size, he thought the humps were as big as large beehives. They were distinctly rounded on top.

Dundee Courier - Monday 21 January 1935

MONSTER SEEN BY PRIESTS
Humps Twelve Feet Apart

The Loch Ness monster gave a half hour's display on Saturday.

It was seen by two Benedictine fathers, several lay brothers, and three boys of the Abbey Schools, Fort-Augustus.

Father Alphonsus O'Connel, an American priest, said in an interview that he watched the monster through an Admiralty telescope. Three humps were in view, each about a foot high. He is convinced that the creature must be large and quite unlike anything he had ever seen before. He thought its speed was about six miles an hour.

Doubter Convinced

Father Sole said he had been sceptical regarding the monster, but what he had just seen proved that the loch did harbour a strange creature.

The object showed three humps which would suddenly merge into two, and then again only one long black object would be seen. The humps were 10 to 12 feet apart, and the total length of the creature was 30 feet or more. No head or tail was seen. He thought the humps were as big as large beehives. They were distinctly rounded on top.

Aberdeen Journal - Monday 21 January 1935

MONSTER SEEN BY MONKS.
Now Convinced That Loch Has Strange Denizen.
HUMPS AS BIG AS LARGE BEEHIVES.

Two Benedictine fathers, several lay brothers, and three boys of the Abbey schools, Fort-Augustus, had a rare thrill about noon on Saturday when they watched from the grounds of St. Benedict's Abbey the Loch Ness monster disport itself at the west end of the loch for over half an hour.

The witnesses are Father Alphonsus O'Connell, an American priest of New York City; Father Bernard Sole, of Banbury, Oxfordshire, who has spent eight years at Fort-Augustus Abbey; Brothers Paul O'Callagan, Magnus O'Brien, Pascal McLachlan, Joseph McAulay, Patrick Collen, John Condon, and Tom Barry, Glasgow; Peter Mohan, Glasgow; and Dick Kelly, Edinburgh, the last three being college boys.

In an interview with a "Press and Journal" correspondent, Father O'Connell said that he watched the monster through an Admiralty telescope, which is guaranteed up to ten miles.

Three Humps Showing

The creature first appeared off the Inchnacardoch side of the loch, crossed slowly towards the opposite shore a mile away, turned east in the direction of the Horse Shoe, and then came towards Fort-Augustus.

Three humps were in view, each about a foot high.

Previously he had not placed much faith in the reports of the monster's existence, but he is now convinced that the creature must be of very large dimensions and quite unlike anything he had ever seen.

He thought its speed was about six miles an hour.

Father Sole stated that, frankly, he had been quite sceptical regarding the existence of the monster or any strange creature in Loch Ness, and, like Father O'Connell, he put the so-called appearances down to rowing boats, motor boats or even ducks flitting about the surface when the light was uncertain.

Strange Denizen.

The living creature he had just seen, however, proved that the loch does harbour a strange animal which is neither seal nor otter. At times, he continued, the object showed three humps.

Each hump he had no hesitation in saying was ten to twelve feet distant from its neighbour, and as all were certainly joined together, the total length was thirty feet or more. No head or tail was seen.

The humps were as big as large beehives. They were distinctly rounded on top.

When last seen the creature was near the mouth of Glendoe Burn.

The loch was calm all the time.

Dundee Evening Telegraph - Thursday 07 February 1935

The Monster Again
Dark-Coloured - And Humped

The Loch Ness monster made a brief appearance at the Fort Augustus end of the loch to-day.

It was seen for several minutes by Mr Duncan Ross, of Drynachan, Invergarry, who is employed as chauffeur-gardener at the Inverness County Sanatorium, and Mr Meldrum, of the Sanatorium.

They were motoring through Fort Augustus, and when crossing the Oich Bridge, the former noticed a huge dark-coloured object rise to the surface near the entrance to the Caledonian Canal.

In an interview they said the object they saw was certainly of huge dimensions, for over five feet of its back protruded above the water. It moved slowly for a short distance, and then plunged out of sight.

It was only a short distance from the shore.

Mr Ross, who has often motored along Loch Ness side, said he had never seen anything like it before. The creature's back, he added, was decidedly humped.

Nottingham Evening Post - Saturday 16 February 1935

LOCH NESS MONSTER RETURNS TO LIFE. FAMILY CLAIM TO HAVE SEEN IT AT PLAY.

An Invermoriston family claim that they saw the Loch Ness monster gambolling in the loch yards from the shore.

Mrs. Stewart, wife of Mr. John Stewart, head gardener to Captain Grant, of Invermoriston, said she saw it from her home.

She called her husband and two sons, and they watched the monster, which appeared to be 30 feet long, frisking about in the shallow water as if it was at play.

"It looked like a huge caterpillar," she said.

Mr. Stewart said the monster threw clouds of spray seven or eight feet above the water. Then it dived, reappeared two minutes later, and finally plunged out of sight, leaving a whirlpool behind it. Altogether the creature was visible for five minutes.

Mr. Stewart added that hitherto he and his family had been sceptical about the monster's existence.

Dundee Courier - Saturday 16 February 1935

MONSTER SEEN AT PLAY
Like Giant Caterpillar

The Loch Ness monster gave a fine display at Invermoriston, slightly east of where the River Moriston falls into the loch.

Only 40 yards from the shore, it was watched by Mr John Stewart, head gardener to Captain Grant, of Glenmoriston, his wife, and their sons, Edward and John.

Their house overlooks the loch, and from it Mrs Stewart first noticed the monster, which, she told a reporter, seemed to be at play, calling the others. It splashed briskly on the surface.

Unlike other parts of the loch, the water there is quite shallow.

Mr Stewart said the creature, which was fully 30 feet long, moved with a definite up and down motion, while his wife described it as being like an enormous caterpillar.

Mr Stewart said the monster threw up clouds of spray seven or eight feet high, and for this reason it was impossible to say how many humps it had. Then it dived with a great splash, reappeared two minutes later, and finally plunged out of sight.

Aberdeen Journal - Monday 22 April 1935

LOCH MONSTER REAPPEARS.
Creature Tempted by Easter Sunshine?
"IT WAS NO SEAL" SAYS WITNESS.

After having lain low for nine weeks to a day the Loch Ness monster made a reappearance at Primrose Bay, near Invermoriston, on Good Friday, when, witnesses declare, "it lay basking on the surface in the glorious sunshine."

The weather was certainly delightfully fine, and in view of the stormy conditions prevailing throughout the greater part of its period of inactivity, this explanation for its long absence seems reasonable enough.

In any case it was watched on this occasion for fully twenty minutes, an unusually long period for the creature to show itself.

Conditions Ideal.

The witnesses were Mrs Scott, wife of Mr Walter Scott, forestry worker, Primrose Bay; their son-in-law, Mr James Riley; and his wife. Mr Riley belongs to Glasgow, his home being 14 Northcroft Road, Springburn.

They said that the object appeared about 2.30 p.m. less than two hundred yards from the shore, and at a point where their house overlooks the loch. The conditions being ideal, the monster creature moved about slowly for twenty minutes.

"It Was No Seal."

The body was thirty feet long and the head they saw was smallish and not unlike that of a seal, "but," Mr Riley said, "it was not seal. Seals do not grow to length of thirty feet, and it is certain that all of the body was not visible."

Dundee Courier - Monday 22 April 1935

The Monster Wakes Up
Easter Appearance in Loch Ness

After having lain low for nine weeks, the Loch Ness monster made an appearance at Primrose Bay, near Invermoriston, on Good Friday.

The monster was seen by Mrs Scott, wife of Mr Walter Scott, forestry worker, Primrose Bay; their son-in-law, Mr James Riley, and his wife.

Mr Riley belongs to Glasgow, his home being at 14 Northcroft Road, Springburn.

They stated the object appeared about 7.30 p.m. less than 200 yards from the shore. Conditions were ideal, and they watched it move slowly about for 20 minutes.

The body was 30 feet long, and the head smallish, not unlike that of seal, but Mr Riley said it was no seal. Seals do not grow to a length of 30 feet, and it is certain all the body was not visible.

The neck tapered like that of a serpent, but it was not raised very high except when the creature prepared to plunge out of sight. The colour was dark brown.

The calm waters, the witnesses added, were churned up when the huge beast dived.

Aberdeen Journal - Friday 26 April 1935

LOCH NESS MONSTER REAPPEARS.
With Black Hump Three Feet High.

The Loch Ness monster made another appearance near Invermoriston, where it was seen by Mr Bartlett Henderson, a young electrical engineer from Inverness, whose firm has a contract the district.

In an interview, Mr Henderson said the monster's form as it rose to the surface and later disappeared reminded him of a porpoise with which creatures he is perfectly familiar, having seen scores them in Inverness firth.

Not a Porpoise.

"Yet," witness continued, "it was certainly not a porpoise, whose peculiar cart-wheeling motions cannot be mistaken, even at a distance."

The black hump, he thought, was three feet high and six feet long.

He called to other workmen in the building but by the time they arrived the monster dived out of sight, leaving a distinct wash on the calm surface.

There was bright sunshine at the time and visibility was perfect.

Dundee Evening Telegraph - Thursday 02 May 1935

Another Monster
SEEN BY CREW OF DUNDEE STEAMER
"Hump-Backed"

There are queer fish in the sea besides the Loch Ness Monster.

The crew of the D. P. & L. steamer Louga, which arrived at Dundee Harbour this morning, have been making friends with one of them.

On several occasions members of the crew have seen a strange sea monster swimming about. It has always been sighted in the same vicinity - near the Longstone Lighthouse on the Fame Islands, off the Northumberland Coast.

On this trip they looked for the strange creature but did not see him.

On occasion they have seen the monster a quarter of a mile from the ship. They describe it as a large hump-backed creature with a longish neck and a small head.

Western Morning News - Friday 03 May 1935

'SEA MONSTER' VISITOR
What Four Cornish People Saw
"GOOSE NECK AND HUMPED BACK"
Fishermen Sceptics At Port Isaac

Lazily gliding around in a smooth sea off the Cornish north coast is what is described as "a monstrous glossy black creature, with long goose-like neck, a humped back, and a tremendous tail."

It has been seen by and has excited four Port Isaac people, and they declare that it is a second Loch Ness monster - if the first existed. It has been seen on three distinctly separate occasions.

On Wednesday morning a young guest-house proprietress was sitting on the top of the cliffs south of Port Isaac looking out to sea. Like people do on a sunny morning she was thinking of nothing in particular, when she saw a huge black monster gliding over the glistening blue sea.

About 1½ hours later another woman was looking out over the charming bay of Port Isaac when she saw what appeared to be a black boat. Not long afterwards a postman was delivering his letters, still a little farther up the coast, when he saw what appeared to be a monster from out of a story book. It was smoothly cutting through the calm waters like a yacht at the foot of the cliff directly below him.

POSTMAN'S STORY
"Going Along Just Like A Yacht"

Here is the graphic description given by Mr. S. J. Honey, temporary postman, of 6, Tintagel-terrace, Port Isaac, to a "Western Morning News" representative yesterday.

"I was delivering my letters at Castle Rock, and was standing at the door of Miss Edith Donnithorne's house, when I looked down to the sea and then exclaimed: 'There is the Loch Ness monster.' Miss Donnithorne looked too, and exclaimed: 'So it is,' and ran for her field glasses. I saw a monstrous thing. It had a big head just like a seal's, a goose-like neck, which must have been standing at least four feet out of the water, and there was a huge hump on its back resembling a big barrel. Floating behind on the surface of the water was a tremendous tail, tapering to a point.

"The creature was between 30ft. and 40ft. length. From the edge of the Castle Rock one could have jumped on to its back. It was going along smoothly, just like a yacht, heading for Port Cavern, and unfortunately going away from me. Then it suddenly sank.

"There was no wash or dive, it just went down flat. I was watching it for quite five minutes, and in the beautifully clear light I could see the sun shining on its glossy black body."

TREATED AS A JOKE.

Mr. Honey is hon. secretary of Port Isaac British Legion. He was emphatic that he was a teetotaller. His father was a fisherman, and he was reared by the sea. "I have seen all kinds of fish in 40 years at sea, and I have never seen the like of this monster before. It was no fish, and more resembled a large amphibian," he declared.

Mr. Honey frankly admitted that he was excited. "Practically everyone I have told has treated it as joke, but I swear by it. If I had been at the bottom of the cliff near by I would have run away."

Mrs. F. E. South, proprietress of the Tre-Pol-Pen Guest House, Port Isaac, said: "I was sitting on the top of the cliff about 11 o'clock on Wednesday morning between Port Quin and Port Isaac when I saw what I thought to a very strange boat. It was of funny shape and extremely black, but I do not think there were many boats out from Port Quin, and thought it rather unusual. Then I thought no more about it until I saw Mr. Honey in the afternoon. The thing was about a quarter of a mile from where I was sitting, and was travelling towards Port Isaac." Mrs. South was born in Suffolk, and is not acquainted with boats.

RUSHED FOR HER GLASSES.

Miss Edith Donnithorne, of the Castle Rock View Private Hotel, Port, Isaac, said her attention was attracted to the creature by Mr. Honey, and she rushed for her glasses. She thought the creature was going to get on to the rocks, from which the screaming gulls hastily flew in fright.

"I am certain it was not a porpoise or a seal. It was a huge black monster, and glided smoothly and steadily towards the rocks. It seemed to know where it wanted to go, and maintained the same speed. It had fins, which makes me think it was not a shark, and it was not the shape of a whale.

"I waited for half an hour after it had disappeared, but did not see it again. It was a most frightening thing. I had never seen such a creature before, although I was born at Port Isaac."

Mrs. Borne, of Mount Pleasant, Port Isaac, was looking out over the bay from her garden about 12:30 when she saw what she thought was a sinking boat. She said it seemed like a boat half submerged, with a man standing on the end. She was not sure what it was exactly, and also thought it might have been a crabbing boat.

Fishermen were at sea on Wednesday waiting for the tide to get to their moorings, but did not see the creature. Coast-guards at Port Isaac station, too, did not see anything out of the ordinary, and the volunteer lookout man at Boscastle has not seen anything. Fishermen of Port Isaac are rather sceptical. They wanted to see the creature with their own eyes before they believed.

Western Morning News - Saturday 04 May 1935

NO SIGN OF MONSTER
Search By Cornish Fishermen
HAS IT GONE UP CHANNEL?
Thought To Be Heading For N. Devon Waters

As they drifted over the calm Atlantic Ocean off the coast of North Cornwall yesterday Port Isaac Fishermen not only sought shell-fish, but also "a monstrous glossy black creature, which has a long goose-like neck, a humped back, and a tremendous tail," but it was not to be seen.

It was (as stated in "The Western Morning News" yesterday) seen by four Port Isaac people on Wednesday.

Mr. S. J. Honey, Port Isaac temporary postman, perhaps saw more of it than anyone else, for it passed directly below him. As it cut its way through the placid sea like a yacht the creature reminded him of artists' impressions of the mysterious Loch Ness monster.

Before it suddenly sank he was able see that it was between 30 and 40ft. in length, that it had a big head, and a huge hump, as big as a barrel on its back.

FROM LOCH NESS?

Port Isaac folk yesterday discussed the curious creature and whether it was a second Loch Ness monster or whether the first monster had wandered away from Loch Ness. They wondered, too, if Port Isaac would have a monster of its own.

But since the monster sank near the rocks between Port Isaac and Port Cavern it has not been seen.

It was obviously making its way up the coast. It might now be off the coast of North Devon. It might have glided past Boscastle and Bude, and might make a "call" at Westward Ho, Ilfracombe, or leave the deep sea for some secluded river.

WAS IT A SHARK?
Opinion At Plymouth Marine Biological Laboratory

Officials at the Marine Biological Laboratory, Plymouth, yesterday were inclined to think that the monster was either a basking shark or a thresher shark.

"Basking sharks are frequently mistaken for sea monsters," an official said. "In this case probably two were together, and the tail tin of one of them sticking above the water might give the impression of a long neck. They are frequently met with off the Cornish coast, and are quite harmless.

"It may also have been thresher shark, although they are more rarely met with. This shark has a long tail, which in this case might tally with the monstrous tail.

"It is, of course, impossible," he emphasizes, "to tell without having seen the thing and thereby gaining a more or less accurate impression of what it looked like."

Nelson's "New Age Encyclopaedia" states that among the characteristics by which sharks may be recognized are "the firm, round tapering body, with projecting snout and unsymmetrical tail." The basking shark is described as reaching a great length - frequently 40 feet - and "is a lazy, inoffensive creature, and an occasional visitor to British seas."

NEED OF INFORMATION
Evidence That Sea-Monsters Do Exist

The story of the sea-monster sighted off the North Cornish coast, by four Port Isaac people should not be regarded as ridiculous.

On the contrary, it should be viewed seriously, and all available information collected.

Lieut.Com. B. T. Gould. R.N., in his book "The Case for the Sea-Serpent," states it as a proven fact that such creatures as sea-monsters while rarely seen and few in number, do actually exist. He has recorded a formidable array of actual observations.

One of the examples be cites as evidence proving the existence the creatures is the experience of men aboard H.M. corvette Daedalus, which arrived at Plymouth on October 4, 1848, bringing with her a story of a strange sea-creature seen in the Atlantic on a passage from the East Indies.

The report made by the captain at the request of the Admiralty was that in latitude of 24deg. 44min. south, and longitude 9deg. 22min. east, something very unusual was seen rapidly approaching the ship from the beam.

"On our attention being called to the object, it was discovered to be an enormous serpent, with head and shoulders kept about 4ft. constantly above the surface of the sea, and as nearly as we could approximate by comparing it with the length of what our main topsail would show in the water there was at the very least 60ft. of the animal a fleur d'eau, no portion of which was, to our perception, used in propelling it through the water either by vertical or horizontal undulation."

Summarizing all the evidence, Lieut.Com. Gould's opinion is that the monster seen at intervals for several decades now has much the same characteristics - a slender neck and tail and a comparatively large body with propelling flippers. Its colour is dark brown above and lighter below, its skin smooth, and some specimens probably possess a mane. Its principal habitat is the Atlantic Ocean, both North and South, and it is migratory.

No sign of the monster has been seen around the north coast of Cornwall in the vicinity of Bude. The coast-guard on duty at Bude from 5 to 10 o'clock last night stated that visibility was very good, but that he had seen nothing unusual in the waters.

Sunderland Daily Echo and Shipping Gazette - Monday 06 May 1935

SEA MONSTER KILLED
"TWIN BROTHER OF LOCH NESS DENIZEN"

A sea monster, twin brother of the famous Loch Ness denizen, has been killed of Mutton Island Lighthouse, Galway Bay.

Fishermen reported that a monster had got entangled in their nets, and after pulling their boat for some distance, struggled free, leaving the nets in shreds.

Five shots were fired at it and the "acquatic King Kong" leapt from the sea, lashing the water in its death agony.

John Crowley, the lighthouse-keeper, had fired the shots, and he said that he had spotted it from the lighthouse and rushed to the beach armed with a rifle.

The monster was 48ft. long and 26ft. in circumference. It has an enormous head and a long scaly body ending in two knife-edged tails.

Experts agree that it belongs neither to the shark nor whale families.

Aberdeen Journal - Friday 24 May 1935

THE MONSTER IS SEEN AGAIN.
Larger Than Fishing Boats Used on Loch Ness.

After another disappearing spell the Loch Ness "monster" was seen at Fort-Augustus yesterday morning.

Mr George Clark, Malvern House, Fort-Augustus, who is district superintendent of the Caledonian Canal, told a "Press and Journal" representative that the "Monster" had two large humps with a distinct hollow curve between and that, altogether, it was considerably longer than the 16ft. salmon fishing boats used on Loch Ness.

It appeared off the old railway pier, and having watched it a few minutes Mr Clark entered his house for a telescope.

When he came out the "monster" had vanished.

No Longer Sceptical.

The humps, Mr Clark added, were dark-coloured and must have been several feet above water.

Previous to this Mr Clark had been sceptical of the "Monster's" existence. Now he is certain that the loch holds some strange creature.

Aberdeen Journal - Saturday 25 May 1935

ANOTHER VIEW OF LOCH MONSTER.
Seen by Man Who Saw it Twenty Years Ago.

Following a brief appearance at the Fort-Augustus end, Loch Ness, at 7.15 a.m. on Thursday, the monster was seen about an hour later in Glenurquhart Bay by Mr Alexander Ross, piermaster, Temple Pier, Glenurquhart, whose house overlooks the loch.

On this occasion the monster gave a thrilling display.

One of the witnesses, Mr Duncan Fraser, Bunloit, Glenurquhart, said to a Press correspondent that the head and neck, and almost the whole length of the monster's body was visible as it careered along the surface in the direction of Urquhart Castle.

It turned inshore and, making for the spot where the Enrick runs into the loch, and where the bay is deeper, it plunged out of sight with a terrible splash.

The body from end to end was, he thought, fully nine feet long, the head not unlike that of a sheep, though much bigger, and the neck long and slender. The creature all over was of a blackish colour.

Twenty Years Ago.

Mr Ross, who claims to have seen the monster over twenty years ago, has some interesting theories about it. When asked if he could explain the reason for its apparent shyness in recent months, he said that in his view the creature disliked coming to the surface in the early months of the year, at which period there are far too many motor boats on the loch for its liking.

Western Morning News - Thursday 06 June 1935

SEA MONSTER NEAR NEWQUAY
"At Least Twenty- Five Feet Long"
HUGE HUMP AND A LONG TAIL
Visitor's Suggestion Of Trapping In Net

Eye-witness descriptions of the strange marine monster which during the last few days has visited the swiftly-flowing waters of the River Gannel, Newquay, suggest that it is similar or perhaps the same creature that was recently seen by four people off the rugged coast of Port Isaac.

Singular features of the creature which has visited Newquay are that on each occasion it has followed practically the same route and procedure, that each time it has invaded the winding river the water has been rough, and the tide high.

It has been plainly seen by at least three people, and each has given the same description, and is convinced that it is not a shark, seal, or any common inhabitant of the sea.

SEEN FROM GARDEN.

Mr. R. H. Northey, proprietor of the Fern Pit Tea Gardens, Pentire, was the first to see it.

On Saturday evening about 7 o'clock he was with his brother-in-law. Mr. S. Morcom. Descending his garden path, which is immediately above the waters of the river, he was surprised to see the 25ft. monster come gliding up the river on the full spring tide. It went a quarter of the mile beyond his gardens and then in a pool about 16 feet deep it suddenly sank. Mr. Northey and Mr. Morcom waited, watching keenly the swiftly flowing river.

Seven or eight minutes later they saw the huge creature practically beneath where they were standing, making towards the open sea at a fast speed.

GOING LIKE SUBMARINE.

"The water was disturbed considerably, and we could hear the wash lapping against the rocks," Mr. Northey told a "Western Morning News" reporter last evening.

"It was at least 25ft. to 30ft. long. At first I thought it was a seal, but a second glance convinced me it was something absolutely different. It was so black and glossy. Its head, several times bigger than a man's, was just above the water. On its back was an extremely huge hump, and flowing behind was a long tail.

"The strange creature resembled an artist's impression of the Loch Ness Monster. It was going just like a submarine on top of the water, and its speed was very fast."

It is interesting to note that Mr. Northey's description compares with that given of the Port Isaac monster. The creature's actions, too, are similar.

There are several mullet in the pool in which the creature submerged, and Mr. Northey thought that perhaps it wanted to get them for food.

WATER DISTURBED.

On Sunday evening Mr. Northey was watching for it again at high tide, when it suddenly appeared from the direction of the sea and repeated the performance.

A visitor, who for professional reasons would not divulge his name, was with Mr. Northey on Sunday night.

The visitor, a friend of Mr. Northey, said, "I looked out for it on Monday and last night. I did not actually see it, but I am sure it came up the river, for there was a disturbance on the water as if some big moving object was making its way beneath the surface.

"I had my glasses and I could hear the water splashing against the rocks. About ten minutes later there was the same disturbance of the water, but this time the submerged creature appeared to be making towards the sea."

The visitor, who declared himself a keen angler, was emphatic that the creature he saw on Sunday evening was not one of the three young seals which recently have been playing off the headland, and said its head was nothing like that of a seal.

He considered it would be possible to capture the creature if a strong net was set and properly manoeuvred.

High tide at Newquay last evening was at 8.20, and although Mr. Northey kept a look-out for the monster there was no sign of it.

Dundee Courier - Wednesday 12 June 1935

Monster Wants to Escape
Seen in Loch Dochfour

The Loch Ness monster, according to the latest evidence, is trying to escape.

It was seen in Loch Dochfour, which is a continuation of Loch Ness, by Mrs Gerald McGrath and her son, Reginald, aged eight.

Mrs McGrath, who is a daughter of Dr Giovannia Hellenoim, of Milan, is on holiday at Fort-Augustus, where her son is a student at the Abbey School.

In an interview she said that she and her son were returning by car from Inverness when the monster appeared. Together they watched the weird-looking creature as it moved slowly towards the chain ferry at Dochfour.

The long, thin neck and small head were several feet above water, and from the monster's back protruded two distinct rows of finlike excrescences, several feet apart.

Mrs McGrath feels certain that the creature is trying to escape.

Aberdeen Journal - Wednesday 12 June 1935

MOTHER AND SON SEE MONSTER.
Is Creature Trying to Escape?

The Loch Ness "Monster" was seen in Loch Dochfour, which is really a continuation of Loch Ness, yesterday afternoon.

It was watched for several minutes by Mrs Gerald McGrath and her son Reginald (8). The boy is a student in the Abbey School, Fort-Augustus, at which town his mother is at present on holiday.

In an interview she said that she and her son were returning by car from Inverness when the "Monster" appeared.

Her son noticed it first and, together, they watched the weird-looking creature as it moved slowly towards the Chain Ferry at Dochfour.

Long Neck - Small Head.

The long, thin neck and small head were several feet above the water.

The creature was less than a hundred yards off the roadway which runs close to the water.

Mrs McGrath feels certain the creature is trying to escape, and added that up till now she had never believed that the "Monster" existed.

Aberdeen Journal - Wednesday 19 June 1935

MONSTER AGAIN EMERGES. CHURNING WATER OF LOCH NESS.

The Loch Ness monster has made another appearance, on this occasion below Glendoe Lodge, Fort-Augustus.

It was seen Mr Robert Forbes, manager of Inverness plumbing firm's branch at Drumnadrochit, and Frank Davidson, Inverness, an apprentice plumber.

They were working at Glendoe Lodge, which overlooks the loch and at a point where the private drive leading to the lodge rises 200 feet directly above the loch.

They saw the creature's huge hack emerge above the calm, sunlit-water close inshore.

"What struck most," declared Mr Forbes, "was the monster's great size. Thirty feet of its sloping back, which was distinctly brown in colour, were clearly visible, and what I took to be a fin or flipper kept churning the water.

"The back at its widest point was several feet across," Mr Forbes continued, "and judging by what I saw the monster's body is easily as thick in the middle as that of an elephant."

Yorkshire Evening Post - Wednesday 26 June 1935

LOCH NESS MONSTER SEEN BY ANGLER.
Said to Have Head Like a Horse.

It has been learned in Inverness that Mr. A. J. Gray, chauffeur, Foyers, while out fishing on Loch Ness at Foyers, had an excellent view of the Loch Ness Monster.

Mr. Gray, in an interview with a "Scotsman" correspondent, said he saw the monster moving about the loch for more than 35 minutes. Other three people whom he summoned also had a view for a part of that time.

"I was about 20 yards out in the loch," said Mr. Gray, "when I suddenly saw a big black object rise out of the water, about 100 yards further out, in the deeper part of the loch. It was the back of the monster. Shortly after, the head and neck appeared, rising from 18 inches to two feet out of the water. Behind I saw quite plainly a series of what appeared to be small ridges, seven in number, apparently belonging to the tail of the creature, which now and again caused much commotion in the water.

"The head was like a horse's, but not as large as that of a horse. It was rather small in relation to the huge body, which was of a slatey-black colour.

"Extremely Heavy"

"From the way the creature moved in the water, I have not the slightest doubt that it was extremely heavy. In moving, it gave a sort of lurch forward, which seemed to carry it about four yards at a time.

"As I watched it, the monster started to go across the loch. I got out of the water with all the haste I could in heavy waders, and then walked along to the Post Office, about 400 yards distant, and informed Mrs. Cameron, who, along with the gardener and a friend hurried to the lochside. We all saw the monster farther out in the loch, but its head and tail were no longer visible. The monster, which had gone out to near the middle of the loch, then turned and came towards the shore again. It came within 200 yards of where we were standing before it set off in the direction of Invermoriston, where it passed out of sight."

Mr. Gray added that he had seen the monster four times before.

Derby Daily Telegraph - Saturday 06 July 1935

DERBY MAN SEES THE LOCH NESS MONSTER – TWICE
"HUMPS" IN THE WATER
MYSTERY OF THE CREATURE WITH "HORSE'S HEAD"

Hitherto I have always regarded stories of the Loch Ness Monster with "a pinch of salt," as the saying goes (writes a "Telegraph" representative), but after interviewing a Derby man to-day I am almost convinced that such a monster does exist.

Here are the facts as given to me by Mr. G. L. Glew, of 56, Friargate, Derby, who, with Mr. H. T. Hicks, of Friargate, has been spending a holiday at the Foyers hotel, which overlooks the loch.

Mr. Glew arrived at the hotel a fortnight ago to-day, and within a few hours had seen the Monster.

"Before I went up there I did not believe a word of this thing," he confessed to me to-day, "but one cannot disbelieve the evidence of one's eyes."

THROUGH BINOCULARS

Mr. Glew explained that on the Saturday evening he was looking through binoculars at the Half Way House, which is situated on the opposite side of the loch, about 4 miles away on the Fort Augustus road.

"The loch was quite calm," he said, "when suddenly something appeared in the water in my range of vision. It was a hump, which moved along the water and disappeared, to be followed by another hump. This came into prominence, and disappeared."

Mr. Glew added that he called the manager of the hotel, Mr. G. W. Lyall, who also saw the humps. Mr. Lyall has lived in the district for several years, and had previously always regarded stories of the monster with suspicion.

SEEN AGAIN

But that is not all. Last Saturday Mr. Glew and others staying at the hotel saw the monster again. It crossed the loch to a dark patch of water in the shade of some trees, and its movements were watched for some time.

Mr. Glew drove in a car to the spot near where the monster disappeared, but could see nothing more.

Others in the district around the Foyers Hotel reported on Sunday that they had seen the monster, which had "a horse's head and seven humps," last Saturday evening.

The problem still remains – "What is it?"

Sunday Post - Sunday 14 July 1935

LOCH NESS MONSTER
Disports Itself Near Yacht

One of the finest views of the Loch Ness Monster was got yesterday afternoon by Captain Wm. George Hewison, who belongs to Whitby, Yorkshire.

Mr and Mrs Hardy, Ilkley, Yorks, two passengers in a yacht the Highlander, which was lying at Temple Pier, Glenurquhart, also saw the monster.

The captain has been at sea for over thirty years, and when interviewed yesterday afternoon by a "Sunday Post" representative on his arrival from Loch Ness, he was quite excited about his experience.

"I have," he said, "had many queer experiences during my long life at sea, but I have never seen anything like the creature I saw moving on Loch Ness.

"It is no ordinary fish, but something of a freak of nature.

"The creature had a definite form but its huge body and its undulating movements were that of the eel tribe.

"I had a clear view of the creature for five minutes through binoculars, and I can saw with certainty that the Loch Ness monster is no joke.

"I was," continued the captain, "below in the yacht in the act of shaving when I happened to look out of one of the small windows.

"My attention was drawn to a very large black object moving about in the water apparently working its way down the loch towards Inverness.

"I dashed on deck and informed my two passengers.

"We at once procured binoculars and I could easily discern something strange moving rapidly in the Loch. It was in full view for about five minutes.

"It had three humps which I saw now and again appearing on the top of the water.

"I would take it to be about 30 feet in length."

Nottingham Evening Post - Monday 15 July 1935

LOCH MONSTER A MONGREL?
Sea Captain's New Theory
ANOTHER APPEARANCE

Just as the Scottish holiday season is approaching its zenith the Loch Ness monster is reported to have made another, and most opportune, appearance.

Capt. William George Hewison, of Whitby, master of the yacht Highlander, believes that it is a freak of nature, a mongrel sea serpent about 30 feet long.

He saw it, he says, from his yacht, which is anchored at Temple Pier, Drumnadrochit, and his evidence is corroborated by two the yacht's passengers, Mr. and Mrs. Hardy, of Ilkley, who watched it for three minutes through binoculars.

Like Huge Eel.

"I was shaving in my cabin," said Capt. Hewison yesterday, "and from one of the windows I had a clear view of the monster. I could see it swimming towards the Inverness end of the loch.

"It moved with an undulating movement like eel on the surface of the water, which gave it the appearance of having three humps."

Capt. Hewison said he had seen many strange things in a long seafaring experience, but he had never seen anything like the monster.

"It is not an ordinary fish at all," he added. "It is something of a freak of nature, but no joke. It is very real. I saw it with my own eyes and I am not easily deceived."

Dundee Courier - Saturday 20 July 1935

LETHAM MAN SEES THE MONSTER
MANY MOTORISTS STOP TO WATCH.

While motoring in the North, Mr W. Hean, of the Commercial Inn, The Square, Letham (Angus), got a glimpse of the Loch Ness monster.

He saw it when motoring along the side of the loch. A long line of cars drew up.

Through a pair of field glasses Mr Hean got a good look at the monster before it disappeared, leaving a wash. He describes it as having a thin head and neck and two humps.

Sunday Post - Sunday 21 July 1935

GLASGOW PARTY SEES NESSIE
"Thought Monster Was Boat At First"

Several Glasgow people touring the North by motor-car got a brief view of the Loch Ness Monster yesterday afternoon between the Halfway House and Invermoriston.

There were five persons in the car, Mr Paterson, the Glasgow garage owner, Mrs Paterson, Mr A. Murray, and Miss A. Murray, of 54 Sunnyside Drive, Clarkston, Busby, and Mr Robert Harrison, of Blairbeg, Drumnadrochit.

Mr Murray and Mr Harrison told a "Sunday Post" representative that they saw a large black object which they momentarily took to be a motorboat with something sticking up near one end.

It made across towards the Foyers side of the loch.

Their view being interrupted by trees they raced the car on to a nearby open space but quickly scanning the water not a trace of the Monster was visible.

At that moment another car arrived and one of the women in it ran forward and told the Glasgow people that her party had also seen the Monster some 100 yards further back.

Thrill For Kilsyth Holiday-makers

Holiday-makers from Kilsyth had also an excellent view of the Loch Ness monster. They watched it bask on the calm surface only a hundred yards from the Canal lighthouse.

The witnesses were Mr Thomas Clelland and his sister, Miss May Clelland, M.A., who are holidaying in Fort-Augustus.

Aberdeen Journal - Monday 22 July 1935

MONSTER BASKING ON LOCH NESS.
"Strong Resemblance to a Huge Eel."

Two holiday-makers, a brother and sister, from Kilsyth, Stirlingshire, had an excellent view of the Loch Ness monster, when they watched it bask on the calm surface only 100 yards from the canal lighthouse.

The witnesses, Mr Thomas Clelland and Miss May Clelland, who are holidaying in Fort Augustus with their parents, said that three humps, a long slender neck, small head and something which resembled part of a tail were clearly visible.

There was a strong resemblance to a huge eel as the creature moved off slowly towards Inchnacardoch Bay.

Mr Clelland thought the body was twenty feet long, and his sister, who is a teacher in Carron School, Falkirk, said – "We were surprised at the small disturbance the monster made in the water."

It vanished quietly beyond the old Tail way pier, heading, they thought, for the nearby bay.

Aberdeen Journal - Friday 26 July 1935

The Loch Ness Monster.

Sir, - With reference to the account in the "Press and Journal" of 22nd inst., an account of an *Aquatilis Bestia,* or aquatic monster, is given on p. 36-38 in Huyshe's book on Adamnan's St Columba, where it tells of some aquatic monster having seized and savagely bit a lad when swimming in the river Ness, whose body was rescued by some men in a boat. It made a second rush at another man but was prevented by the command of a Saint.

According to Dr Reeves, certain rivers and lakes were haunted by serpents of a demoniacal and terrible character in Ireland – "the dreadful beast, the wurran, half fish half dragon" - seldom seen but often heard.

Our Loch Ness monster must the descendant, as St Columba lived A.D. 521-600. - Yours, etc., Alice Forbes. Brux Lodge, Alford.

Dundee Courier - Tuesday 06 August 1935

MONSTER SHOWS OFF TO U.S. VISITOR
1½ Miles in Two Minutes

Two visitors to the district, one of whom came specially to look for it, saw the Loch Ness monster at the weekend.

The Very Rev Dr Thomas Moore, an American priest from Washington, who is staying at St Benedict's Abbey, saw the creature from the abbey grounds at 9.30 in the morning.

The abbey grounds offer splendid opportunity for viewing Loch Ness, and Dr Moore said that he saw two large humps break the calm, sunlit waters. Then the monster moved off towards Corrie's Cave.

"The creature followed a semi-circular route, and disappeared below the surface just beyond the rocky cliff at the cave,' he said.

'It left a clearly-defined wash, and my only regret is that I did not have my telephoto cine-camera with me.

'The humps were several feet apart, and the creature travelled over 1½ miles in about two minutes while I watched."

The other witness was Major Phillips, Basingstoke, whose perseverance was rewarded with A view of the elusive creature. He saw it near Invermoriston.

Aberdeen Journal - Monday 19 August 1935

LOCH NESS MONSTER
Seen by Steamer Crew and Passengers.
TEN MINUTES' VIEW GOT.

Captain, officers, members of the crew and many passengers on the Loch Ness pleasure steamer Gondolier got a ten minutes' view of the Loch Ness monster.

The vessel was crossing the Loch about 10.40 a.m. between Foyers Pier and Altsigh House, which is on the opposite north shore.

Captain Peter Grant told a Press representative that a large black hum was observed travelling at a fair speed almost in the middle of the Loch.

The creature was witnessed by most of those on board and some of them watched it through telescopes and binoculars. Among the observers was Sir Edward Campbell, M.P.

Captain Grant stated that he and several of the crew saw the monster on two occasions last summer, and in his opinion its bulk and general appearance show it to be something very uncommon, for he has never seen the like in salt water or fresh.

Altogether the monster was under observation for ten minutes. The wash it created was a notable feature of the appearance.

Nottingham Evening Post - Monday 19 August 1935

MONSTER SEEN AGAIN.
LOCH NESS SHIP'S CAPTAIN'S THIRD VIEW.

Among the latest people who have seen the Loch Monster are Sir Edward Campbell, M.P., and Captain Peter Grant, who is in command of the Royal Mail steamer Gondolier. The ship runs dally between Inverness and Fort William.

It was while on the westward journey on Friday morning, when the ship was rounding Foyers Point, that the monster showed its back. Captain Grant told a correspondent on Saturday that he, several of the officers and crew, and a number of passengers, including Sir Edward Campbell, who was touring the Highlands, watched the creature plough through the water with part of its back showing for 10 minutes.

The creature, he said, created a distinct wash and although this is the third occasion on which he has seen it, he has no clue to its identity. Judging by its bulk and movements, he said, he has never seen anything resembling it either in salt water or fresh.

Burnley Express - Wednesday 21 August 1935

The Chief Constable of Preston (Mr. J. P. K. Watson) claim to have seen the Loch Ness "monster." His description of it is that the "monster" is 25 to 30 feet long, has two large humps and a small head. Mr. Watson has been on holiday in Scotland.

Dundee Evening Telegraph - Thursday 22 August 1935

MONSTER SEEN BY GIRLS
Head Like That of Cow

Twenty feet of the Loch Ness monster's body, the head, and what was thought to be the tail, were clearly seen by two maids employed by Mr F. M. S Grant of Knockie, at Knockie Lodge, Whitebridge, Stratherrick.

In an interview they said they watched the creature from 7 p.m. till 7.30, and during that time it disappeared below the water only once, and came to the surface almost immediately.

The girls are Miss Molly Stewart, who belongs to Invermoriston, and Miss Rae Grant, whose home is at Foyers.

Miss Giant said that in the evening her companion and herself took a walk to the top of the hill which overlooks Loch Ness, and from it they were gazing down on the, calm, sunlit waters, when the monster appeared, almost directly below, at a distance of only a few hundred feet. "First," Miss Grant said, "what seemed be the creature's tail emerged, lashing the water: then up came the head, which was something like a cow's, but kind of oval-shaped and smaller." The total length of the dark-coloured body was, she thought, twenty feet.

They watched it disport itself under perfect conditions, and when they departed it was still splashing about the on surface, near Knockie boathouse, and quite close to the shore.

Dundee Courier - Saturday 24 August 1935

SEARCHING FOR THE MONSTER

Count Adrian Bentinck of Overvean, Holland, a distinguished scientist, is at present at Half-Way House, Inverness-shire, with his family. The Count is deeply interested in the Loch Ness monster, of which he has had a distant view. Photo shows the Count with his wife, Countess Jacoba, and his daughter, Countess Louise.

Aberdeen Journal - Monday 09 September 1935

BLASTS SCARE MONSTER?

The Loch Ness monster was seen by Mrs Watt, wife of Mr George Watt, the retired Sheriff-Principal, of Drumbuie, Glen Urquhart, and her daughter, Miss Joyce Watt, while they were motoring to Inverness.

Mrs Watt, in an interview, said that she saw four or five humps, and her daughter thought there were six or seven.

The monster appeared, they said, a mile east of Temple Pier, and it was splashing a good deal, and not moving fast.

The splashing made observation difficult and, to get a better view, they drove on some distance.

At the next vantage point, however, a [???] showed that the creature had disappeared.

Mrs Watt believes the monster has been a very long time in the Loch, and that the reason for its unusual activity these past two or three years can be traced to the huge amount of rock blasting done while road construction work was being carried along the Loch side.

Second Appearance

Another appearance was reported from the east end of the Loch, near Dures village, where the monster was seen by three people motoring towards inverness.

They were Mr R Stone, a chauffeur from London, who is employed by the tenant of Killin Shootings, Stratherrick, a cook, Mrs Bird, also from London, and employed at the same address, and a friend.

They stated that they saw a large, dark coloured body emerge near the Dores side, and travel up the Loch at a fast speed.

The creature moved with a lurching motion, and for five minutes they had it under observation.

What impressed them most was the heavy wash it created, the Loch being quite calm.

Previous to seeing for themselves, these two witnesses ridiculed the Loch Ness monster's existence.

Dundee Courier - Tuesday 24 December 1935

SIREN SCARES NESS MONSTER
Woman Watches It for Ten Minutes

The Loch Ness monster has been seen again after four months' "retirement." A young woman watched the creature's gambols for 10 minutes.

Miss Rena Mackenzie, daughter of Mr and Mrs Wm. Mackenzie, who live near Invermoriston pier, said that while walking along the lochside about three o'clock in the afternoon she saw the monster's head and neck rise from the calm surface. It moved slowly along, quite close to the shore.

The head was small in comparison to the length and thickness of the neck, Miss Mackenzie said, and what struck her most forcibly was that the under part of the neck was white.

After she had watched it for five minutes a steamer siren startled the creature, for, after turning its head "in an agitated manner," it plunged out of sight.

Miss Mackenzie saw it reappear, and watched it for another five minutes, when it set off quickly for the opposite shore. The head was about four feet above water level.

Four months have elapsed since the Loch Ness monster was seen near Urquhart Castle by Mrs Watt, wife of Sheriff-Principal Watt (retired), Drumnadrochit.

1936

Nottingham Evening Post - Tuesday 24 March 1936

THE MONSTER AGAIN.
LOCH NESS VISITOR'S CLOSE DESCRIPTION.

After a lapse of three months the Loch Ness monster made its appearance on Sunday afternoon, when the loch was as calm as a mill pond.

The observer was Mr. Alpin Chisholm, ex-Mayor of Morris, Manitoba, Canada, who is visiting friends in Glen Urquhart after an absence of almost 50 years.

With his niece, Miss Marjory Mackenzie, of Douglas-row, Inverness, he was motoring above the loch at Lower Bunloit Glen, Urquhart, when he saw a large creature emerge out of the water about a third of a mile from Inverfarigaig on the opposite side of the loch.

"The creature seemed to be heading for the bay at Glen Urquhart Castle," said Mr. Chisholm.

"It did not show abnormal speed or any unusual disturbance in the water. Its neck seemed long, and projected forward, having a faint resemblance to a racehorse in action.

"The neck and a great part of the head seemed rough and ugly, and was apparently either flabby or covered with matted hair.

"The beast remained on the surface for over two minutes, and just as I was focussing a camera on the spot it disappeared.

"I estimate the length of the beast at about 30 feet."

Aberdeen Journal - Tuesday 24 March 1936

The Monster Returns

The Loch Ness monster may be a survival from a remote age in antiquity, but he has nothing to learn from a modern advertising agent. This winter, when driving snow and plentiful wreaths isolated the Highlands, he lay low and hibernated in the Loch's primeval mud over Christmas. But with the vernal influences at work again, he is up and doing in good time for the Easter vacation. His appearances last year showed approximation to the public holidays that could not have been mere coincidence. By some means he has procured a pocket diary and knows when people are free to come to the shores of Loch Ness and look for him. It may be that his power of attraction is failing, but his technique is improving. He studies his public and does his level best to whet their curiosity. For that assiduity in local patriotism and his devotion to duty, if for nothing else, he deserves to go down in history with General Wade and Walter Scott as a populariser of the Highlands.

Aberdeen Journal - Tuesday 24 March 1936

MONSTER COMES UP AGAIN
Seen by Holidaymaker in Glen Urquhart

After a lapse of three months the Loch Ness monster made its appearance on Sunday afternoon when the loch was as calm as a mill pond.

The observers were Mr Alpin Chisholm, former Mayor of Morris, Manitoba, Canada, who is home on holiday visiting his friends in Glen Urquhart after an absence of almost fifty years.

Along with his niece, Miss Marjory Mackenzie, Douglas Row, Inverness, he was motoring at a point above the loch Lower Bunloit, Glen Urquhart, when he saw a large creature emerge out of the water about a third of a mile from Inverfarigaig village, on the opposite side of the loch.

Heading for Bay

The creature seemed to heading, said Mr Chisholm, for the bay at Glen Urquhart Castle.

It did not show abnormal speed nor any unusual disturbance in the water. Its neck seemed long and projected forward, having a faint resemblance to a racehorse in action. The neck and a great part of the head seemed rough and ugly, and apparently either flabby or covered with matted hair.

"The beast remained on the surface for over two minutes, and just as I was focussing a camera on the spot it disappeared.

Doubt Vanishes

"I estimate the length of the beast about thirty feet. I only arrived," said Mr Chisholm, " in my native glen a few days ago, and I was sceptical of the existence of the monster. All doubt has now vanished, and I am certain that there is in the loch a creature that is large and mysterious."

Dundee Courier - Saturday 28 March 1936

The Loch Ness Crocodile
Monster Comes Inshore for Close-Up Study

The Loch Ness monster is now reported to have a head resembling that of a crocodile.

A party of Inverness ladies who were motoring along Loch Ness-side had a closeup view of the monster in the vicinity of Glenurquhart Bay.

The party included Mrs Grant, of Ardlarich, Inverness, and her son, Douglas, and Mrs Munro, Ashton, near Inverness, and Mrs John Maciver, Victoria Terrace, Inverness.

Mrs Grant said they were motoring from Balnain along the lochside when they saw the monster less than a hundred and fifty yards away.

"Enormous Head"

"An enormous head was protruding from the water," said Mrs Grant, "and a long wash was created by the creature's body.

"The head was not unlike that of a crocodile, many of which I have seen in India. The monster was swimming complacently, not at any great speed, when it curved out of its course and made towards the shore.

"I sounded the motor horn several times but the monster carried on unruffled. It was still swimming on serenely when we left."

Dundee Courier - Monday 20 April 1936

Students See The Monster
It "Snorted" and Made a Heavy "Wash"

Three Glasgow University students - Robert Fairweather, Samuel Hall, and J. Yaggo - walking from Inverness, told the warden at the youth hostel at Glen Nevis on Saturday night that they had seen the Loch Ness monster.

They said that, while resting behind a large boulder at the lochside, about five miles from Fort-Augustus, they heard a loud snorting noise, and they saw a black-scaled creature coming towards the shore at a great speed.

"It came to within about fifty yards of the shore when, as if sensing danger, it suddenly turned and made a dash for the middle of the loch," one student stated.

"It's body was about thirty feet in length, and it had a snake-like head and small eyes.

"It travelled at a great speed, setting up a heavy wash and making a noise like a paddle steamer.

"Its body had an undulating motion, which gave it the appearance of having three humps. It remained above the surface for about ten minutes."

The students were unable to photograph it, as they had used their last spool.

Western Daily Press - Tuesday 21 April 1936

EYES ON LOCH NESS

Having remained quiescent for some two years the Loch Ness monster is said to be once more on the prowl. On Saturday three Glasgow University students reported that they had seen an apparition resembling in all material respects the prodigy whose intervention enabled Scotland to weather the economic blizzard more comfortably than many feared. Reclining languidly on the banks of the Loch, the students were startled from their meditations by a violent snorting accompanied by a noise like a paddle steamer in motion. Starting up they saw black-scaled creature with snake-like head and small glittering eyes approaching land at a great speed. Its three hump s rose and fell rhythmically as it raced along, and its passage set up a heavy wash as it made for the shore. What would have happened if the monster had not noticed that spectators were present there is no knowing. With fifty yards still to go it became suspicious; its suspicions turned to certainty, and with a tremendous heave it turned in its tracks and retreated incontinently into the middle of the loch. There is no gainsaying that this sudden reappearance happens at an opportune time when the holiday season is about to begin, and when the departure of the Queen Mary has created a void in the excitements of Scotland which needs badly to be filled. It is conceivable, of course, that the students were mistaken, that what they saw was not the authentic monster but the figment of some fantastic dream to which they had succumbed. As for that, the obvious course is to wait and see whether the vision will be vouchsafed to someone else. Though little is known about the habits of the Loch Ness monster, it has never failed to exhibit itself at intervals once the rumour of its presence had leaked abroad. If this practice is maintained we may expect a series of exciting visitations during the months that lie ahead. Up to now the monster has been shy and elusive, and all efforts to entice him to close quarters have failed. What is needed in Loch Ness, as it is needed elsewhere, is the spirit of confidence, so that with a little coaxing the monstrosity may swim about unconcernedly on the surface and pose without self-consciousness for the films. But how to create this happy spirit so necessary for men and monsters? Scotland might fairly be expected to make a contribution by prohibiting fishing in the Loch or by warning off would-be aggressors. For its part the monster might respond by renouncing violent tactics and by appearing more frequently in public than has been its wont. By such simple beginnings there might be built up a cordial understanding and a spirit of mutual forbearance which could not fail to be beneficial to all concerned. Naturally such a development cannot be realised in a moment. A preparatory period is essential during which overtures could be exchanged and the way paved for a comprehensive conciliation. The fact that the monster has approached to within fifty yards of the shore before taking fright is itself a good sign. With a little tact and perseverance it may shortly be feeding out of our hands.

Dundee Courier - Thursday 30 April 1936

NESS MONSTER SHOWS ITSELF AGAIN

The Loch Ness monster was seen yesterday morning by a London commercial traveller who was motoring from Inverness to Drumnadrochit. He is Mr Provost, Scottish representative of a London firm.

When he was opposite the north end of the loch his attention was attracted by a huge dark-coloured creature which was travelling at high speed towards the far side of the loch. He watched it for several minutes, and saw that it caused a great disturbance in the water. The loch was fairly choppy, but Mr Provost had no difficulty in following the creature's movements for nearly two miles.

Western Daily Press - Wednesday 13 May 1936

Another Loch Ness Monster?

An extraordinary thing happened here (a Clevedon correspondent writes) on Monday afternoon. I was strolling down Alexandra Road towards the sea front when I suddenly and distinctly beheld in the sea near the pier a very queer creature. It had a long thick neck many feet in length and two large humps on its back, also a tail which threshed the water. After 1 had watched it for a quarter of an hour it submerged itself. It answers to the same description as the Loch Ness monster. Perhaps some subterranean disturbance has affected these creatures, perhaps relics of prehistoric times. May I add this is not the only occasion have witnessed this strange thing in the water here, and always in the neighbourhood of the pier. Other persons than myself have observed the strange creature.

Dundee Courier - Friday 19 June 1936

Loch Ness Monster Again

After a lengthy period of inactivity the Loch Ness monster was seen near Urquhart Castle yesterday.

Two of the witnesses are commercial travellers and reside in Inverness. They are Wm. S. Matheson, of 18 India Street, and Cyril Scott, who represents Messrs Crawford, biscuit manufacturers, Edinburgh.

Mr Matheson said that when he was motoring from Inverness to Fort-Augustus, and at a point two miles east of Drumnadrochit, he noticed the monster emerge above the calm sunlit water. It travelled, he said, with a distinct rolling motion towards the Inverness end of the loch at a terrific speed, sending out great volumes of waves and spray.

Suddenly it dived, came up again, then, heading this time for the Fort-Augustus end of the loch, it repeated its display of diving and speed.

Mr Matheson and Mr Scott had a perfect view of the monster's two large shiny humps for between five and ten minutes.

A short time previously the monster was seen opposite Foyers by Mr Duncan McMillan, Lennie Cottage, Drumnadrochit, and a family of tinkers.

Aberdeen Journal - Monday 22 June 1936

MONSTER AT PLAY
Seen by Rover Scouts at Loch Ness
HAD THICK NECK LIKE SEAL

Twelve young Inverness men camping at Dores, about six miles from Inverness, watched the gambols of the Loch Ness monster in the water for half-an-hour yesterday morning.

All the men were members of the patrol leaders' training camp organised by the 3rd Inverness Crown Troop of Rover Scouts.

Scoutmaster Alan Macpherson and Assistant Scoutmaster John Macleod and Alexander Mackenzie were the first to notice the monster about 10.30.

Great "Wash"

They were standing on the shore of the loch when one of them pointed out an object on the surface of the water about a mile and a half away. At first it was thought that the object was a canoe, and for about five minutes no further attention was paid to it.

When the three Rovers looked again, however, they observed that the object had travelled about half a mile nearer them, and was now within a mile of where they were standing.

It was making a great wash as it moved by what appeared to be flappers at its side.

Realising that the monster was making one of its infrequent appearances, the other three members of the camp were hurriedly called, and one of them brought a pair of powerful binoculars. For about half an hour the Rovers watched the monster's antics, each of them having a turn at looking with the binoculars.

Thick Neck Like Seal

A graphic account of the monster's appearance was given to the "Press and Journal" representative by A.S.M. John Macleod, who, with other members of the camp, returned to Inverness last night.

"The monster - and I have not the slightest doubt but that was what saw," said Mr Macleod, "was gambolling in the water on the Invermoristou side of the loch when we first saw it. When it came closer and we were able to train binoculars on it, we were able to get a perfect view.

"It is difficult to give an estimate of the monster's length, because there was nothing else on the surface with which to compare it, but we saw quite clearly that the monster had a thick neck like a seal.

"As it moved over the surface of the water the back wash was heavy, and I saw that the flappers at its side, which assisted its progress, apparently caused the wash.

"The people who have described it as being like an upturned boat have given a good description of it, for it appeared to us like that also. After we had watched it for about half-an-hour, it disappeared into the depths of the loch."

Aberdeen Journal - Thursday 25 June 1936

"MONSTER" SEEN AT SEA
Experience of Fraserburgh Crew

Has the monster escaped from Loch Ness?

A denizen of the deep, the description of which is similar to that of the creature that has been disporting itself in the Highland loch for the past two years was seen at the fishing grounds by two Fraserburgh steam drifters.

The skipper of the Coral Bank (FR12) gave a "Press and Journal" representative the following account of the incident:

"We had reached the fishing ground of Little Bank, and decided to shoot our nets there, 41 miles N.N.E. from Kinnaird Head.

"From the wheelhouse I saw what I took to be a tree floating on the surface, with stumps all over it. I called attention to it so that the nets might not be fouled when being shot.

"Members of the crew at the stern called back that it was a big fish of a kind they had never seen before.

"It closely resembled," said the skipper, "the appearance of the pictures of the Loch Ness monster I had seen in the newspapers. The creature was following the herring, and came within ten feet of our stern so that we all had a good look at it.

"About sixteen feet of its length showed above the water, but the swirl it made, although it did not seem at all alarmed by the proximity of the boat, indicated that it was much longer.

"The creature had three humps on its back, had a long neck and a head like a camel of a greyish hue. When the shooting of the nets began the monster disappeared under the boat."

All the other nine members of the crew corroborated the skipper's narrative.

After leaving the Coral Bank the creature swam past the bow of the drifter Verdure (FR557), which was in the next berth. A member of the crew of that boat substantiated what had been said by the skipper of the Coral Bank.

Aberdeen Journal - Saturday 04 July 1936

THE MONSTER HAS LONG SWIM
Queue of Motorists Watch Its Progress

Scores of people had an excellent view of the Loch Ness monster yesterday forenoon, when it appeared near Dores and stayed above the surface of the water for nearly hour.

It first made its appearance shortly after nine o'clock and motorists and tourists travelling along the Glen Albyn Road drove their cars into the side the road and watched the monster to their hearts' content.

At one time there were as many as fifty cars at the side of the road near Temple Pier.

Residents in houses alongside of the loch left their homes to view the monster.

Mr J. Stevenson of Brackla, whose home is within sight of the loch, told a "Press and Journal" representative that he was one of the first to notice the monster.

He estimated its length to be about twenty to thirty feet, and it had two humps. It was at times rather like two rowing boats. It travelled at a fair speed and created a noticeable wash as it moved.

Dundee Courier - Monday 10 August 1936

THE SEA SERPENT.

The Loch Ness monster seems to have been inactive and retiring this summer or its news value has fallen off.

It may prove a stimulant to it to hear that a sea monster apparently its own type has been sighted by highly respectable witnesses within a mile of the Norfolk coast. The witnesses were a former Lord Mayor of Norwich, a former M.P., and a former Parliamentary Secretary to the Admiralty.

The Norfolk monster had all the characteristics of Drumnadrochit's kelpie - humps and curves above the water surface, a long neck, and a terrific speed, estimated by the ex-Mayor, the ex-M.P., and the ex-Admiralty official at from 90 to 100 miles per hour. The last is presumably a good judge of nautical performance.

If the Loch Ness monster is not promptly reported from its favourite haunts a suspicion is bound to go abroad that it has abandoned them and gone for a sea voyage. Perhaps it has been moved by a nostalgia and a longing for the taste of sea water.

In such a summer as this the water Loch Ness must have grown fresher and fresher.

Nottingham Evening Post - Friday 14 August 1936

ARE THERE TWO MONSTERS? LOCH OICH VISITORS GET A CLOSE-UP.

Has the Loch Ness monster migrated, or has it a relative in the adjoining Loch Oich?

This question has arisen as a result of an extraordinary story of the appearance in Loch Oich of a creature which closely resembles the Loch Ness monster.

Alderman A. J. Richards, headmaster of Evydale-road Public School, London, his son, Mr. J. A. Richards, and friend, Mr. G. M. Wilkinson, of London, were boating at the Laggan, end of Loch Oich on Tuesday afternoon when they saw a weird-looking creature emerge from the waters.

First two humps, like the coils of a snake, appeared only dozen yards from the boat.

Then the head appeared, and so close were the astounded witnesses that they could see it was shaggy and like that of a dog.

Alderman Richards said he had never believed in the Loch Ness monster, but now he is convinced that the Highlands lochs harbour animals which are unknown to zoologists.

Loch Ness and Loch Oich are connected by a river forming part of the Caledonian Canal.

Dundee Courier - Friday 14 August 1936

ANOTHER MONSTER.

Veracious and credible witnesses, one of them an Alderman - who could be no more suspected of leg-pulling than a Bailie - are to-day testifying to the appearance of a monster of the now familiar yet elusive type in Loch Oich.

It has the usual humps and shaggy head, but it is not the Loch Ness monster, for it is less than half that interesting creature's length.

According to local authority, this creature has been seen on and off in bygone years, but the observers have been remarkably reticent about it. Probably more favour will given to the conjecture that the Loch Oich monster is the offspring of the Loch Ness monster, even though the theory requires two Loch Ness monsters for its full validity. This presents no difficulty. The descriptions of the Loch Ness monster have varied sufficiently to allow of half a dozen, and the fact that they have never been seen in company would merely mean that monsters are not gregarious. For the human inhabitants of the great Caledonian valley that is perhaps just as well.

Loch Oich is connected with Loch Ness by the River Oich, up which young monsters might travel with ease. As it is a much smaller and shallower loch than Loch Ness the study of its monster inhabitant is more promising. An expedition from the zoological departments of the Scottish universities is clearly indicated as the right thing.

Dundee Courier - Friday 14 August 1936

Monster Bobs Up: In Loch Oich
Startles Men In Boat
Serpent Coils and Shaggy Head

The story of the appearance in Loch Oich, Inverness-shire of a creature which closely resembles the Loch Ness monster was given yesterday by Alderman A. J. Richards, a member of Camberwell Borough Council and headmaster of Evydale Road Public School, London.

Other witnesses were his son, Mr J. A. Richards, and a friend, Mr G. M. Wilkinson, of Frest Holme, Queen's Road, Forest Hill, London.

They were boating the Laggan end of Loch Oich early on Tuesday afternoon when they saw a weird creature emerge from the water, at that point only a few feet deep.

First two humps, like the coils of a snake, appeared only a dozen yards from the boat. Then the head appeared.

SHAGGY HEAD.

So close were the astounded witnesses that they could see it was shaggy and like that of a dog.

The creature kept diving and reappearing, first one coil being seen, then both, followed by the head, which was shaken vigorously each time it came up.

The coils, which were three feet high by the same length, appeared about three feet apart, with the head the same distance away, so that the total length of the creature was over 12 feet. The monster was speedy in its movements.

Mr Richards, jun., who is about 20 years of age, said the creature's nearness to the boat gave them all an uneasy feeling, and he rowed for the shore. There he waited for the monster to reappear, but it did not do so.

Alderman Richards said they had never believed in the Loch Ness monster's existence, but now he was convinced that those Highland lochs harboured a race of animals which were quite unknown to zoologists.

The colour of the "humps" and head, he added, was almost black, the former reminding him of a snake.

Like the Loch Ness monster, our Fort-Augustus correspondent states, this creature has been seen on and off in bygone years, and the descriptions given by various witnesses still living correspond in most respects with that given by Alderman Richards, his son. and Mr Wilkinson.

Mr Richards, his wife and family, whose home is at 169 Court Lane, Dulwich, are at present on holiday at Invergarry Station.

Loch Oich lies in the Great Glen, between Loch Ness and Loch Lochy.

Hull Daily Mail - Saturday 15 August 1936

THAT SEA SERPENT

Various opinions are expressed as to the possible explanations of the Withernsea sea serpent. Flights of ducks, schools of porpoises, grampuses are all suggested. Some scoffers ask if those who claim to have seen it have just come from a banquet!

But too many make the claim for there to be any doubt that they have seen something unusual. Yet might not the truth be that what they have seen is really a sea serpent?

Few people deny that there was something real to justify the Loch Ness monster. It moved extremely fast, and if in Loch Ness, why not the bay between Flamborough Head and Spurn?"

After all, the sea bed is a huge uncharted area to us, and there are many mysteries in its unfathomable depths that we have still to solve. Might not the Withernsea monster be one of those?

If it has done nothing else the Withernsea spectacle has given us all something interesting to talk about and speculate on, and that, in these "silly season" high summer days, is an achievement for even a sea serpent be proud about.

Aberdeen Journal - Monday 24 August 1936

LOCH NESS MONSTER PUTS IN APPEARANCE
Sceptical Londoner Convinced

The Loch Ness monster, perhaps looking to its laurels in view of the opposition monsters that have appeared in Loch Oich and at Orkney, made a brief appearance off Foyers on Saturday.

Its observers on this occasion were Mr and Mrs K. Inger of 150 Sutherland Avenue, Maida Vale, London. Mr and Mrs Inger are on a motoring holiday and were travelling towards Inverness, near Temple Pier, when the monster made its appearance nearly half a mile out on the loch about seven o'clock in the evening.

Speaking to a "Press and Journal" representative, Mr Inger said the monster remained in sight for about ten minutes. He estimated its length to be at least thirty feet and two large humps showed distinctly, well above the water. A considerable wash was made by the monster's movements but throughout its appearance it did not seem to shift far from the one place.

"Like many Londoners," said Mr Inger, "I was doubtful of the monster's existence, but I am now quite satisfied that Loch Ness has a unique creature in its depths."

Aberdeen Journal - Saturday 12 September 1936

MONSTER SEEN FOUR TIMES
Three Humps, Long Neck and Small Head

A motoring party from Fort William got a fine view of the "monster" in Loch Ness.

The calm surface of the loch was suddenly disturbed about 400 yards from the shore, and the party were amazed to see three large humps appearing, followed in a few seconds by a long neck and small head.

The beast appeared four times and was visible for fully ten minutes. It was proceeding along the loch at a great, pace, and was followed for about a quarter-of-a-mile by the ear.

The viable part of the animal was fully fifteen feet long, and to the rear appeared be a tail, which was not visible, but which set up a strong, lashing movement, causing a tremendous disturbance in the water.

Dundee Courier - Saturday 12 September 1936

Monster Reappears in Old Haunts

Contrary to the fears of the dwellers on Loch Ness side, the monster has not deserted the old haunts there for the neighbouring waters of Loch Oich.

A motoring party from Fort-William, Mr Ian Mackintosh, solicitor, Troon, accompanied by his wife and her father, Mr Donald Livingstone, contractor, Fort-William, viewed the creature yesterday while traversing the road along the side of Loch Ness. Mrs Mackintosh remarked that it was an ideal day for seeing the monster, as it was dead calm. On previous holiday visits to Fort-William they had always been disappointed.

Then they noticed a disturbance on the calm surface, which gave the impression that a squall had ruffled the water. They were amazed to see three large humps appear. Later they got glimpses of a long neck and small head.

The creature was about 400 yards from the shore, and was visible for ten minutes.

It was proceeding along the loch at a great pace, and Mr Mackintosh kept abreast of it for a quarter of a mile in the car.

The visible part of the animal was 15 feet long, and to the rear there appeared to be a tail which was not visible, but which set up a strong, lashing movement, causing a tremendous disturbance in the water.

Dundee Courier - Tuesday 22 September 1936

Twin Monsters Now
Close-up of Loch Oich Creature
"Furry" Body; Dog-Like Head

Latest indications are that there are two monsters in the Great Glen - one in Loch Ness and the other in Loch Oich. Both were seen at the week-end.

Two Fort-Augustus brothers, Colin R. Campbell, temporary postman, and Archibald Campbell, draper, were motoring home in the evening, when about 1½ miles from the village they saw two lines of foam on Loch Ness. The disturbance was caused by either one or two objects which scarcely showed above the surface, but were travelling at what they described to our correspondent as "express train" speed.

Two dark-coloured, shiny humps appeared by the time the creature was near a promontory known as Fraser's Point. Continuing its mad rush it disappeared in the direction of Inchnacardoch Bay, which seems to be its favourite haunt.

The brothers say that fully 15 feet separated each hump.

POWERFUL STROKES

The mysterious creature in Loch Oich was seen by Mr Simon Cameron, canal bridge-keeper, Laggan, Invergarry.

The weather was clear, and Mr Cameron said that the creature rose to the surface in the bay beside his house. With quick, powerful strokes of its fore-limbs it travelled briskly in an easterly direction, where it was lost to view. Six feet of its furry-looking body, along with a dog-like head, were clearly visible.

When asked if he thought it might be an otter he replied, "There is no otter on earth anything like that size."

Aberdeen Journal - Tuesday 22 September 1936

MONSTERS ON THE MOVE
Seen Going at 'Express Train Speed'
MAY BE TWO IN LOCH NESS
Powerful Loch Oich Creature

Summer-like weather at the weekend brought the two Highland loch monsters to the surface of their respective haunts.

Two Fort-Augustus brothers, Messrs Colin R. Campbell, temporary postman, and Archibald Campbell, draper, were motoring towards Fort-Augustus in the evening, and when about a mile and a half from the village they noticed two unusual lines of foam on the water.

Keeping watch, they saw that the disturbance was caused by either one or two objects, which scarcely showed above the surface, but were travelling at what they described to our correspondent as "express train speed."

Dark, Shiny Humps

Suddenly, however, two dark-coloured shiny humps appeared close to a promontory known Fraser's Point, and continuing its great rush the creature disappeared in the direction of Inchnacardoch Bay, which seems to be favourite haunt.

The witnesses stated that since fully fifteen feet separated each hump they formed the opinion that there may have been two monsters in the loch. In any case, it will be recalled that the monster or monsters gave a similar display near the same place two years ago, when it was watched by, among others, Sir Duncan and Lady Hay, of Peebles.

When first seen on the present occasion, the monster was less than twenty yards from the shore.

Furry and Doglike Head

The Loch Oich creature was again seen by Mr Simon Cameron, canal bridge keeper, Laggan, Invergarry. The weather for observation was also perfect.

Mr Cameron said in an interview that the animal rose to the surface in the bay beside his house, and with quick powerful strokes of its fore limbs, travelled briskly in an easterly direction, where it was lost to view.

Six feet of its furry-looking body, along with the doglike head, were clearly visible.

Aberdeen Journal - Wednesday 30 September 1936

IN LOCH NESS AGAIN
Monster Seen by 50 People
FINE VIEW GOT OF CREATURE

One of the most remarkable displays yet given by the Loch Ness monster was that witnessed by nearly fifty people one-and-a-half miles west of Urquhart Castle, when the creature, which showed its head, neck and two humps, remained in view for fifteen minutes.

The first person to see the creature was Mr Duncan Macmillan, jun., who has for the past four years been employed by Inverness County Council as road patrolman between Urquhart Castle and Invermoriston, and who is a familiar figure to hundreds of motorists who pass along that part of the Glenalbyn Road. He was standing at his cottage door at Lennie, which occupies a commanding position above the new road overlooking Loch Ness.

Mr Macmillan said that the first thing he saw was the neck and the head, the latter being small and grey in colour. The monster was about halfway out in the Loch, but the calmness of the atmosphere permitted of the creature being seen quite easily with the naked eye.

Mr Macmillan, realising that rarely could the creature be seen to better advantage, called to his wife, who joined him, followed by three men from Dingwall who had just partaken of tea from Mrs Macmillan. The party stood by Mr Duncan Macmillan, the seventy-eight years old father of the first named witness and by Mrs George McKay, a sister Mrs Macmillan, jun., who lives at Scone, Perthshire.

Like Sea Serpent

Slowly, said Mrs Macmillan, the monster moved along with head and neck clearly visible, the head reminding her of pictures she had seen of a sea serpent. Then two distinct humps, black and shiny, appeared, one of them fairly close to the head and' the other some distance behind. Just then two motor cars arrived, followed by two of Messrs Macbrayne's Glasgow and Inverness buses and a motor cycle driven by the A.A. road scout, Mr Bond, Inverness.

A number of people from the cars and buses had cameras and many snapshots were taken, but whether any good pictures were got remains to be seen, as the cameras appeared to be very small. Telescopes and binoculars also were used, but those who had them were too late see the neck and head, which had that time disappeared. Two humps, however, remained view most of the time, she added.

Asked what she was most struck by Mrs George Mackay said that altogether the sight was wonderful. She was greatly impressed by something which was below the surface to the rear of the last hump and fanlike in shape. This part of the monster's body, she said, kept moving from side to side, making a great disturbance and helping, she thought, to propel the huge body along.

Dundee Courier - Wednesday 30 September 1936

Monster's Record "Gate"
50 Watch It Splash
Scone Woman Sees Its Tail

The Loch Ness monster, in one of the most generous displays it has yet given, was seen by nearly 50 people one and a half miles west of Urquhart Castle.

The creature, which showed its head, neck, and two humps, remained in view for 15 minutes.

The first person to see it was Mr Duncan Macmillan, who is employed by Inverness County Council as a road patrolman. He was standing at his cottage door at Lennie.

Mr Macmillan told a reporter that the first thing he saw was the neck and the head, the latter being small and grey in colour. The monster was about halfway out in the loch, but the calmness of the atmosphere permitted of the creature being seen quite easily.

Mr Macmillan called to his wife, and they were joined by three men from Dingwall, who had been having tea at the cottage; Mr Duncan Macmillan, the 78- year-old father of the first-named witness; and by Mrs George McKay, of Queen's Road, Scone, a sister of Mrs Macmillan, jun.

Bus-Loads of Witnesses

Then two motor cars arrived, followed by two buses and an A. A. scout on a motor cycle.

When the head of the monster went under water it did so while the neck was in a vertical position. This seems to be an unusual feature, as in most previous appearances it was particularly noticed that the head and neck were lowered parallel to the water before plunging below.

Mrs George McKay, who is on holiday with the Macmillans, said she noticed something below the surface to the rear of the last hump and fanlike in shape. This part of the monster's body kept moving from side to side, making a great disturbance and helping, she thought, to propel the body.

Her brother-in-law said the disturbance was like that caused by the paddles or propellers of a steamer.

Aberdeen Journal - Thursday 01 October 1936

MONSTER OF LOCH NESS AGAIN
Watched by Artist for Five Minutes

Another appearance by the Loch Ness monster, which seems to revel in the fine weather, was reported yesterday afternoon, this time from the Fort-Augustus end of the loch, where it was watched as it travelled over the greater part of a mile at what the witness described as a terrific speed.

It was seen on this occasion by Miss Jobson, an artist from North Walsham, Norfolk, who is on holiday in Fort-Augustus.

She told a Press representative that she was sitting at the lochside at Borlum Bay, painting a picture, when her attention was drawn to the appearance, near Fraser's Point, of a long thick neck, which suddenly popped out of the water.

The loch was perfectly calm, and visibility was excellent, so Miss Jobson had no difficulty in following the creature's headlong rush as it raced towards the Glendoe side of the loch, about one-and-a-half miles away. All she saw, however, was a long neck and head, which she said seemed to resemble almost exactly those displayed on comic postcards of the monster. What impressed her most, she said, was the great length and thickness of the neck.

Altogether Miss Jobson watched the creature for about five minutes, and when asked at what speed it was moving, she replied that it travelled faster than any speed boat she had ever seen. Miss Jobson said she had always believed in the monster's existence.

Dundee Courier - Monday 26 October 1936

The Monster Has a Frolic
Women Motorists Look On

A party of women who were motoring along Loch Ness-side had a clear view of the monster in the vicinity of Abriachan, several miles from the Inverness End.

The party consisted of Mrs Moir, widow of Dr John Innes Moir, senior medical officer of health, British Honduras; Fiona, her little daughter; Mrs Moir, Aberdeen, her sister-in-law; Miss Fraser, Kenneth Street, Inverness; and Mrs Grant, Ardlarich, Culduthel Road, Inverness, who was driving the motor car.

Mrs Moir, Inverness, in an interview, said – "It was in the late afternoon that we saw the monster. About five to six hundred yards away was a black moving object.

"The creature had three humps, the one in the centre being the most prominent. It was moving in the direction of Inverness. It had a long thin neck. The object suddenly turned and shot straight across some distance to the other side of the loch.

"It proceeded quickly and created a considerable wash as it raced along. It came back to where we had seen it originally.

"We noticed that the humps had disappeared under the water, the creature apparently being either feeding or playing."

Mrs Moir added that when they left the monster was still there. They had watched it for over a quarter of an hour.

Aberdeen Journal - Monday 26 October 1936

THE MONSTER AGAIN
Seen by Inverness and Aberdeen Party
LITTLE GIRL GETS SCARE

The Loch Ness monster was watched by an Inverness motor party disporting itself in the waters of Loch Ness for about ten minutes not far from Foyers.

Although it was getting dark and the water was rough, the witnesses on this occasion - Mrs Grant, Ardclarich, Inverness; Mrs Moir Aberdeen; Miss Fraser, Stafford Lodge, Kenneth Street, Inverness; Mrs J. Innes Moir and her nine-year-old daughter, Eiona, also of Stafford Lodge - had excellent views of the monster.

They described it as a large black creature, with three distinct humps, and a long neck and snake-like head.

Little Eiona Moir got a scare on seeing the monster, and screamed with fright.

Glossy Black

A vivid description of the party's experience was given to a "Press and Journal" representative by Mrs Innes Moir, who returned to this country two months ago from British Honduras, where her husband, the late Mr J. I. Moir, was senior medical officer for the colony.

"We were returning to Inverness," she said, "along the east side of the loch the other day, and spotted the monster about three miles past Foyers. Stopping the car, we got out, and watched it. It would be about five o'clock and the light was fading, and the loch was getting rough. Despite that drawback, we had an excellent view of the creature.

"At first it moved slowly down the loch in the direction of Dores, its glossy black body showing up against the grey coloured waters, and we distinctly saw the three pronounced humps and its snake-like head."

Disporting Itself

Mrs Moir said that after the monster had proceeded some little way down the loch, it returned to where they first saw it, and began disporting itself in very lively manner. It was about 600 yards from them, and they clearly saw the spray it threw up.

Mrs Moir remarked that the monster gave the impression of being a sinuous creature.

"I was always somewhat sceptical of the existence of the monster, but I am now convinced that there is some strange beast in the loch," she concluded.

Falkirk Herald - Wednesday 04 November 1936

LOCH "MONSTER" FILMED
Existence of Animal Claimed to be Established
SCOTS CAMERAMAN'S "SHOTS"

The existence of a "monster" in Loch Ness is finally established, it is claimed, by a film secured by Mr Malcolm Irvine, director of Scottish Film Productions, after an intermittent but persistent search for the animal over a period of more than three years.

The film shows an animal more than 30 feet long travelling through the water at a speed said to be in the region of 30 knots.

Mr Irvine first caught a glimpse of the monster in December, 1933, and he has seen it half a dozen times since then, but it was not until a few weeks ago that he was able to obtain a film record of it.

On Tuesday, September 22, he stationed his assistant cameraman, Martin Wilson, at a point opposite Inverfaragaig, while he himself remained about two miles farther south. Both had cameras fitted with powerful telescopic lenses.

The conditions were ideal for observation, only a slight swell from the south-west and occasional light breezes disturbing the calm surface of the loch.

"A BIOLOGICAL MYSTERY"

At half-past three Mr Irvine caught sight of his quarry coming out of the Foyers side of the loch.

"I packed hurredly," Mr Irvine said in an interview, "and sped around the bay at Invermoriston, stopping at a point about two miles away where we had previously selected a suitable station. I could see the monster with the naked eye, moving swiftly about half a mile away.

"When at last everything was ready to shoot, his line of travel had changed to north-west. I started turning and panning at the same time. It was difficult.

"The great magnification of the telescopic lens which I was using exaggerated every movement, and, try as I would, I could not keep the panning movement uniform.

"I was content, however, to have the monster in the picture and to get what I know to be a unique record of a unique animal.

"The film shows the head and neck parallel with the surface, and rising and falling with the movement of the huge body. The humps are also seen rising and falling gently as the flippers move beneath them. The rudder-like tail is clearly seen."

"What kind of animal do you think it is?" Mr Irvine was asked.

"That," he replied, "is a biological mystery. To place him under any known category is out of the question."

'DOUBTS OF THE SCEPTICS SHATTERED"

Mr Irvine describes the monster as over 30 feet long, dark grey, almost black, in colour, and very shiny.

His description coincides closely with that given by Margaret Munro, of Fort Augustus, the only person who has seen the monster out of the water.

"The monster," she told Mr Irvine, "was up on the beach sunning himself. His long neck and small head were swaying to and fro, while his heavy body was turning over slowly to enjoy the warmth of the sun. He was as long as the Chevalier, and his tail was still in the water." The Chevalier is one of the steamers plying on the Caledonian Canal, and is about 50 feet long.

Experts who have been accorded a private view of the film are agreed that it shows a picture of an animal hitherto unknown to zoologists. Mr Eric Foxon, Fellow of the Linnean Society, which has devoted part of its proceedings to an investigation of the Loch Ness monster, granted Mr Irvine a camera interview after seeing the film.

Mr Foxon declares that the animal does not fall into any known category. The doubts of the sceptics, he says, are shattered. "Henceforward everyone will require to admit that there is something in Loch Ness."

The film of the Loch Ness monster will be shown in cinemas throughout Great Britain this month as a special feature in the first number of Scottish Film Productions' newsreel pictorial, "Things That Happen," produced by Mr Stanley Russell.

Aberdeen Journal - Tuesday 24 November 1936

LOCH NESS MONSTER MAKES REAPPEARANCE
Humps, Tail and "Snake" Head

Two young women cyclists got an excellent view of the Loch Ness monster near Fort-Augustus.

In an interview they told our Fort-Augustus correspondent that while they were returning from Fort-Augustus about 3.45 in the afternoon they saw the monster making a tremendous disturbance on the loch's calm surface about a mile from Fort-Augustus.

Three large, dark-coloured humps, what appeared to be the tail and the snake-like head, were clearly seen, the creature being only about a hundred yards from the shore and travelling fairly fast towards the Inverness end of the loch.

Suddenly, however, the monster changed its course and made for the Glencoe (south) shore, and after crossing it disappeared, this time in the direction of Fort-Augustus.

1937

Aberdeen Journal - Friday 12 February 1937

TEACHERS SEE MONSTER PLAYING ABOUT IN LOCH NESS STRANGE-LIKE CREATURE

After an interval of almost four months the Loch Ness monster was again seen at the Fort-Augustus end of the loch.

It was under observation for nearly half an hour under perfect conditions.

The witnesses were Miss C. A. MacGruer, who belongs to Invermoriston, and Miss Rachel Cameron, whose home is Fort-William. They are teachers in Fort-Augustus School.

SMALL POINTED HEAD

They had gone for a short walk before lunch, soon after 1 p.m., and, after passing Cherry Island, their attention was drawn to the loch by the sudden appearance of the long, powerful neck and small pointed head of a strange looking creature as it swam at a fair speed towards where they stood on the main Inverness-Fort-Augustus road.

The creature, which both witnesses soon realised was none other than the monster, was first noticed near the east end of Inchnacardoch Bay, a favourite haunt.

With a quick rolling motion it rapidly approached the shore, and eventually came to within less than a hundred yards of the roadside.

Keeping perfectly still and quiet for the next twenty-five minutes they had a wonderful view of the monster as it dived, reappeared, turned its head repeatedly, and played about on the surface, thoroughly enjoying, or so it seemed to the onlookers, the gorgeous sunshine.

NOT SEAL

While no actual outline of the body could be seen, the ladies declare that, judging by the thickness and length of the neck, which was usually over three feet above water, and the huge disturbance it made, the body must be of huge proportions, for some part which appeared to cause most of the upheaval was what was described as "a good bit to the rear of the neck."

Both witnesses are absolutely positive that the creature is not a seal, but something quite out of the ordinary. There was a big white spot on the creature's chest.

Finally it swam gently towards Fort- Augustus, less than a mile distant, and disappeared in the bay at the back of St Benedict's Abbey.

Dundee Courier - Tuesday 02 March 1937

Loch Ness Monster Twice Seen Again Enormous - Terrific Upheaval

The Loch Ness monster has been seen again, and on each of the two latest occasions witnesses described the outline of its back resembling an upturned boat.

The monster appeared first near the Half-Way House, two miles east of Invermoriston, when a party motoring to Inverness saw it emerge from the surface about 11 a.m.

The party included Mr and Mrs Frederick Campbell, late of Bankok, Siam, and now residing at Innisslan, Fort-Augustus.

Mr Campbell, who was driving, told our correspondent that, although only the back was in sight, they were astounded at the creature's enormous bulk. Hoping to get a better view, they drove to where the road rises and offers a closer observation-point. But by that time the monster had submerged, leaving scarcely a ripple.

Mr Campbell, who has fished Loch Ness for salmon for about 20 years, said he had never seen the like before, and is completely at a loss to account for a creature of such astonishing size and capable of such high speeds having its home in the loch.

SEEN BY SERVANTS.

By a strange coincidence the monster was watched for several minutes at the Fort-Augustus end of the loch, over ten miles distant, about an hour later by a maid and a gardener employed by Mr Campbell, Innislann - Miss Elizabeth Cameron and Mr Albert J. Thoumine.

The latter saw the monster rise to the surface near Inchnacardoch Bay.

Calling to the maid, he and she watched it, when it seemed to be resting, for almost five minutes.

"Then," Mr Thoumine said, "it seemed to cant forward, probably headfirst, and plunged out of sight amidst a terrific upheaval, the spray being flung high in the air."

Questioned as to the length of the creature's back, Mr Thoumine said it was much longer than a 15-feet salmon fishing-boat, and from four to five feet above the water.

Aberdeen Journal - Tuesday 02 March 1937

MONSTER'S APPEARANCES IN LOCH NESS

The Loch Ness monster made two appearances last week - one near Fort-Augustus and the other opposite the Half-Way House.

On both occasions the weather was ideal for observation, and special interest attaches to the several witnesses' statements, for the strange creature showed only its huge, black, sloping back.

Each of the observers declared that the shape of the body reminded them of "an upturned boat," a description which has been repeatedly given in the past few years.

The spray the monster sent up when it made the plunge out of sight was described as terrific.

Aberdeen Journal - Tuesday 16 March 1937

LOCH NESS MONSTER WATCHED BY TWO STUDENTS NEAR FORT-AUGUSTUS

After last week's storm yesterday's brilliant sunshine is thought to have attracted the Loch Ness Monster to the surface, as it was seen off Johnnie's Point, near Fort-Augustus, early in the afternoon.

The witnesses, Colin McPherson Young, of Aberdeen, and Gerald Patrick Fitzgerald, Glasgow, are young students of the Benedictine Abbey School at Fort-Augustus, and they told our representative that when out walking on the Inverness highway they saw a strange-looking object, with a black, shiny back, appear on the loch's calm surface about 100 yards from the shore.

At first glance the object was like an upturned boat, but presently it began to move off-shore. Then, the witnesses said, they saw its neck and a small, pointed head. When the creature had travelled half-way across the loch it suddenly plunged out of sight.

Altogether the students watched the creature for six minutes.

Aberdeen Journal - Wednesday 31 March 1937

LOCH NESS MONSTER "VINDICATION" BROADCAST TO-NIGHT

A new turn to the controversy about the reality or otherwise of the Loch Ness monster will be given to-night, when Commander R. T. Gould, the authority on sea monsters, will broadcast a "vindication."

For twenty minutes in the London Regional programme he will give listeners fresh facts which, in his opinion, prove the existence of the monster.

His talk is the direct result of a recent broadcast on "sea monsters" by E. G. Boulenger, of the Zoo Aquarium.

Commander Gould wrote to the B.B.C. and his letter was so informative and interesting that he was invited to expand it in the form of a talk. In his letter Commander Gould stated he had five photographs of the Loch Ness monster.

He also revealed the fact that he had statements and drawings from two friends who had observed it. These friends are Captain F. E. B. Haselfoot, R.N., a naval surveyor, who saw the monster for fifteen minutes at a range of 400 yards, and Professor A. W. Stewart, Belfast University.

Dundee Evening Telegraph - Thursday 01 April 1937

LOCH NESS MONSTER IS NO JOKE

The Loch Ness "monster" is no joke. Commander R. T. Gould, in a broadcast on "Sea Monsters" last night said that it would be possible for a large sea creature to enter the Loch by way of the River Ness when it was in spate, and the creature would find there sufficient salmon and other fish to feed half a dozen monsters.

The creature has proved by no means a nine-days'-wonder, Commander Gould declared. In each of the years 1933-1936 it has been sighted on more than 20 separate occasions, and has been reported already four times this year.

Photographs, films, sketches, and the statements of eye-witnesses concerning the monster bore one another out. he said, and disposed of the suggestion that it was a whale, seal, or other creature known to science. It had a long neck, which it lifted only occasionally.

Those who regard the Loch Ness "monster" and sea serpents in general, as an exploded joke, could not have the faintest idea of the overwhelming evidence of their existence, he concluded.

Aberdeen Journal - Saturday 17 April 1937

THE LOCH NESS MONSTER
Monk "Who Knows Most About It" Describes Amphibian to Boys

The Loch Ness monster was yesterday responsible for another mystery in which Aberdeen University figured.

According to a statement reported to have been made by the Right Rev. Sir David Hunter-Blair, eighty-three-year-old monk of the Order of St Benedict's, the monster was filmed about three months ago.

Although not yet released, the report stated, the film would be shown at Aberdeen University next week, and he would speak on the monster at the same performance.

At once interest in the monster transferred from Loch Ness to Aberdeen University. The officials at the University were mystified. They knew nothing about the film, and stated that no arrangements had been made to show it at Marischal College.

NO LIGHT ON SUBJECT

"I cannot throw any light on it at all," said Principal Fyfe when approached on the matter by a "Press and Journal" representative. "I have not heard a word about it."

The Principal suggested humorously that the new professor of Natural History, Professor Hogben, who has just arrived at the University, would no doubt like to have the monster in the natural history museum.

Very naturally some thought the film might be an invention of the students for their Charities Week campaign, but the convener of the Students' Publicity Committee was just as much mystified as Principal Fyfe and everyone else. No such film, he said, was included in their programme.

"SOME CONFUSION"

To clear up the mystery, the "Press and Journal" communicated with Sir David Hunter-Blair in Manchester. He then stated that he did not intend to say that the film was to be shown at Aberdeen University next week. There must have been some confusion. He had read in the Press that a Loch Ness monster film had been made, and would be shown in Aberdeen. If and when he heard of the film being shown there, he would go and see it. He had no arrangement or date for any visit to Aberdeen apart from that.

Sir David is Abbot of Dunfermline and the only living founder of St Bede's Roman Catholic College in Manchester. His reference to the Loch Ness monster was made in a talk to the boys at the college during yesterday's diamond jubilee celebrations.

POST-GLACIAL CREATURE

"I know more about it than anyone else," he declared. "It is an amphibian of the post-glacial period, and I don't believe it belongs to any existing species. It possibly belongs to the Devonian period. There has always been a legend or rumour of a monster at Loch Ness."

Sir David expressed the opinion that the monster's first appearance in 1933 was due to the blasting during road operations on the loch side. But. when it came to the surface, it found good vegetation and very nice food and the hottest weather on record in Scotland. Since then, he said, it had appeared regularly and was seen now about once every fortnight.

Refuting suggestions that the monster could be anything else than an amphibian, Sir David referred to the stories of it being seen on various occasions.

CREDIBLE WITNESSES

"Many people" he said, "call it 'collective hallucination.' This is nonsense. About 200 witnesses have seen it, and those witnesses are by no means all one class.

"The Scottish Highlanders have a reputation of being truth telling people. What they say is true. What they saw was a head with a long face like a horse and grey whiskers, but the whiskers were probably roots which the monster had come to the surface to eat.

The monster has no protective armour like the tortoise. Its body is like snail's - smooth and shiny - and how it manages to live without being crushed by the pressure of the water I don't know. It is, of course, shy and not fierce, although it is now becoming accustomed to people.

"After its first land appearance it left the heather, grass and bracken on the lake side trampled as if a steam roller had passed."

WISHES IT CAUGHT

Referring to its popular appeal, Sir David added: "Hundreds of people come up to Loch Ness and stay at the hotel - which is, of course, a very good thing for the hotel. Music hall comedians and newspapers have made it a joke in London, but people in London get tired of hearing the same joke and, nowadays, you hear nothing of the monster.

In conclusion Sir David remarked: "I am in favour of it being caught."

Aberdeen Journal - Tuesday 20 April 1937

MONSTER SEEN TWICE WITH SHINY, BLACK HUMPS SPEEDING ALONG LOCH NESS

The Loch Ness monster was seen twice during the week-end.

At Inchnacardoch Bay, near Fort-Augustus, it was observed under perfect conditions.

Miss Bella Macrae, who was out walking with the four children of Mr and Mrs Alex. C. McKenzie, The Old King's Inn, Fort-Augustus, with whom she resides, was sitting near Cherry Island when there appeared the monster's black-humped, shiny back, three to four feet out of the water.

It was twenty yards off the island itself, which is only a stone-throw from the shore.

There was also in view a flipper or fin, black and shiny and powerful-looking.

The creature remained on the surface for only a minute or two before plunging out of sight.

Yesterday a correspondent had an interview with other witnesses, who had seen the monster on Saturday but refused to give their names.

A young married couple from Edinburgh were motoring towards Inverness when they saw, near Foyers, what the lady described as two large, shiny humps, a good distance apart, sailing along the surface like an upturned boat at a fast speed in an easterly direction.

"There is no doubt," the lady stated, "that there is something very large and very strange in Loch Ness."

The couple are on holiday at Fort-Augustus with their family.

Aberdeen Journal - Wednesday 09 June 1937

MONSTER AGAIN POPS UP
VERY HIGH SPEED IN LOCH
WAS SHOWING ONE BIG HUMP

The Loch Ness monster, after a seven weeks' absence, made an appearance near Urquhart Castle.

It was seen by two men, one of them a native of the district, and the other a young London cyclist, who is touring the Highlands.

The latter, Mr L. Galvin, stated that while cycling past the castle in the direction of Fort-Augustus, another man on a cycle stopped him and drew his attention to an object in the loch.

"There was no doubt," Mr Galvin said, "that it was the monster, in whose existence I have never believed. However, there it was, showing one big hump and travelling at a very high speed towards the Fort-Augustus end of the loch."

Owing to its speed and the upheaval in the water Mr Galvin said it was impossible to say how many humps were occasionally showing, but he thought there might have been perhaps three altogether.

After watching the creature for two or three minutes it was by that time out of sight.

Mr Galvin said he was highly pleased to have really seen the monster.

Aberdeen Journal - Monday 28 June 1937

BABY MONSTERS IN LOCH NESS SAID TO HAVE BEEN SEEN BY BOYS

Baby monsters are reported to have appeared in Loch Ness.

The story with its implications of a happy monster family life somewhere in the depths of the Loch, comes from two boys aged fourteen and fifteen who are pupils at Fort-Augustus Abbey.

While on the shore of the Loch, near the Abbey, they saw on the surface two creatures which they are convinced were the baby monsters.

Their description of the infants runs – Three feet in length, dark in colour, propelled by four legs, long tapering tails, like big lizards in general appearance.

Aberdeen Journal - Wednesday 14 July 1937

THREE MONSTERS IN LOCH
Observed for Several Minutes

Three "monsters" - a large one and two smaller - were seen together in Loch Ness.

Eight people living in a house overlooking the loch at Brackla, near Abriachan watched the trio at play for more than five minutes.

The party, which included Mr and Mrs A. Stevenson, of Brackla; their two daughters; Mr R. Gourlay, on holiday from Ireland; and Mrs R. Gourlay, jun., of Loanhead, Edinburgh; and Mr S. J. Stevenson, Bristol, were sitting at breakfast when Mr Gourlay, jun., looking out of the window, saw a dark object on the surface of the loch.

TREMENDOUS SPLASHING

"There's the monster," he exclaimed, and immediately the party went to the door of the house and saw a big, black and shiny object.

"The object," said Mr Gourlay to a "Press and Journal" representative yesterday, "was about five feet long and two feet above the surface of the loch.

"We were watching the big monster so intently for about a minute that we failed to see two other objects, one on either side of the big monster.

"From where we stood it was quite easy to hear the splashing of creatures. One of the small monsters travelled away rapidly towards the Foyers shore, and, with a tremendous splashing noise, it disappeared.

"The big monster, together with the other small one, went away towards Urquhart Castle."

FULLY FIVE MINUTES

Mr Gourlay, who said the party watched the creatures for fully five minutes before they all disappeared, added that when the monsters were travelling they created a considerable commotion on the surface of the water.

Mr A. Stevenson, who has lived in the district for many years, said yesterday that never before had he believed in the monster's existence, but now he had no doubt.

Bath Chronicle and Weekly Gazette - Saturday 24 July 1937

SEA MONSTERS OFF SCALPAY
WILTSHIRE OFFICER'S STRANGE STORY

Loch Ness must look to its laurels. Two rivals to the famous "monster" are reported to have been seen off Scalpay Island, near Skye, by Colonel H. R. B. Donne, of Seend, near Devizes, who has just returned from a holiday in the district.

Colonel Donne told a newspaper representative: We were moving from Loch Kishorn to Portree in a small motor-yacht last Friday, and, when nearing a red beacon off Scalpay Island, we saw the first monster.

"There were four bumps, or fins, obviously connected with the same body, and slowly waving in different directions.

"From time to time a fifth bump, apparently indicating a snout, was seen," continued the Colonel.

"It was not much under 40 feet in length.

"Half a mile farther on we saw a second monster, similar to the first, which was still in sight in the distance."

Colonel Donne has a statement describing the occurrence signed by himself, his wife, Mrs. Kitchener, owner of the yacht, and Robert McLachlan the skipper.

Aberdeen Journal - Tuesday 27 July 1937

LOCH MONSTER "SNAPPED" BY YOUNG ABERDEEN STUDENT ALSO SEEN BY FIFE VISITORS

The Loch Ness monster was seen twice at the week-end, and on one of its appearances was "snapped" by William Young, a seventeen-year-old Aberdeen student of the Abbey School, Fort-Augustus.

The photograph was taken as the creature lay on the surface of the water near the Abbey boathouse.

Mr Young, who is one of three brothers at the school - sons of Mr William Young, fine art and antique dealer, 262 Great Western Road, Aberdeen - and has gone for a holiday to Ireland, told a "Press and Journal" correspondent that when he saw the monster showing above the surface he rushed to the school for his camera, but by the time he got back the creature had moved far out of range.

ROWED IN PURSUIT

Nothing daunted, the student ran to the boathouse, launched a dinghy, and rowed off in pursuit.

Three hundred yards out he caught up with the monster, which, however, dived when the picture was about to be taken.

But again the monster came up, and this time was duly "snapped" - and at close range.

Unfortunately, either excitement or the "vile weather" - in Mr Young's own words - marred what would otherwise have been a good picture, but the young man hopes for better luck next time.

He stated that fully five feet of the monster's broad back were above water when he made the exposure, and the skin was grey, and slimy-looking.

LONG PILLAR-LIKE NECK

While motoring towards Fort Augustus, where he is spending a holiday with his wife and two children, Mr L. A. Rolland, chartered architect and surveyor, in business at 47 High Street, Leven, Fife, saw the monster emerge from close inshore a mile east of Invermoriston.

First they saw a long, pillar-like neck and small head very near the shore and quite erect.

Then the creature rushed at terrific speed towards the opposite shore, faster than any motor boat.

What struck witnesses most was that fully ten yards behind the neck there was either a limb or tail which whipped the water into foam and indicated that, tail or limb, it was the motive power behind the creature's mad rush along the surface.

The latter being like glass the wash it created, Mr Rolland said, was like that of a large steamer, and he felt certain that the creature must be enormously powerful and bulky.

Dundee Courier - Tuesday 27 July 1937

STILL GROWING.

The Loch Ness monster appears have been living a more retired life this year than in previous summers, perhaps because, like so many humans, it considers that the holiday climate is not up to the mark.

But it is interesting to note from the narrative of its latest appearance that it is still growing, and is becoming more of a monster than ever.

To the best of our recollection, its wake when swimming on the surface has hitherto been likened to nothing larger than that developed by a motor boat. But as seen by Mr Rolland, of Leven, and his family, "the wash it created was that of a large steamer."

It also seems to be developing a more remarkable organ of propulsion. The "long pillar-like neck and small head" remain as in many previous accounts, but the "limb or tail which whipped the water into foam" and produced the steamer-like wake was fully thirty feet behind the neck, and drove the creature at terrific speed.

All this should encourage the researchers, whose enthusiasm seems to be slackening. The bigger the monster (and its wakes) becomes the better a photographic subject it will make.

Aberdeen Journal - Monday 02 August 1937

THE MONSTER CONVINCES SCEPTICS

Members of the Edinburgh Warriors' cricket team, who are touring the Highlands, got a splendid view of the Loch Ness monster while on their way to Inverness from Fort Augustus during the week-end.

The party were travelling in cars and, when about twelve miles west of Inverness, one of them noticed two black humps breaking the surface of the water about mid-way across the loch.

"TREMENDOUSLY THRILLED"

The party watched the object for several minutes. It was impossible to ascertain whether one of the humps was the monster's head or not, but they saw the object, which looked black and shiny in the evening sunshine, move slowly towards the other side of the loch, creating a considerable wash as it did so.

Mr J. Duthie, who is a member of the party, told a "Press and Journal" representative yesterday that the monster was still visible when they continued their journey.

"Although it was moving slowly it really seemed to be basking on the surface of the water," he said. "The description given by other people about the monster being like an upturned boat coincided with the experience we have had. A few of us had small cameras. Several photographs were taken, but it is unlikely that these will be of any value because the monster was so far away at the time. We were tremendously thrilled at seeing the monster because most of us were previously inclined to disbelieve in its existence."

SERPENT-LIKE HEAD

Our Fort-Augustus correspondent states: For fifty-five minutes the Loch Ness monster was watched, three miles east of Urquhart Castle on Saturday evening by almost 100 people.

Two humps and the head were clearly seen. The distance from the front of the first hump to the rear of the second was between twenty-five and thirty feet. The creature travelled altogether one-and-a-half miles and came slowly across from the Dores side. By and by the head, which an eye-witness described as serpent-like, was seen. It was raised and lowered frequently, also turned to right and left.

Dundee Courier - Monday 02 August 1937

Monster Performs Before a Crowd

The Loch Ness monster "showed off" for 45 minutes before a crowd of about 100 at the week-end.

The scene of the big performance was near Urquhart Castle about six o'clock in the evening, with the sun shining brilliantly.

Mr Peter Grant, Tomdoun Hotel, Glengarry, with his daughter Miss Annie Grant, and son, Mr Allan Grant, and a friend, Mr A. Gillespie, Paisley, were returning by car from Dingwall. They said that never before had they seen so many people assembled at the lochside to watch the monster.

Two humps and the head were clearly seen, and the distance from the front of the first hump to the rear of the second was between 25 and 30 feet. The creature travelled on the surface altogether 1½ miles, coming slowly across the loch from the Dores side towards where the witnesses stood.

Soon the head, which Mr Grant described as "serpent-like," was seen, and seemed to be raised and lowered frequently, and was also turned towards the crowd.

Aberdeen Journal - Saturday 07 August 1937

MONSTER SEEN FOR 35 MINUTES
FIVE HUMPS: BODY 30 FEET LONG

Three Edinburgh business men motoring along Loch Ness side had an excellent view of the Loch Ness monster yesterday.

For thirty-five minutes they saw it move quietly along the surface of the water.

In an interview at Fort-Augustus, they stated that when seven and a half miles east of Fort-Augustus they noticed the monster swimming about on the surface on the Glencoe side.

It appeared, they said, to have been disturbed by the paddle-steamer Gondolier, although of that they could not be certain, but, before it disappeared, the head, neck, and five distinct humps remained clearly in view for almost half an hour.

The neck was eight feet long and the body about thirty feet.

Dundee Courier - Saturday 07 August 1937

Monster Loses Speed

Three Edinburgh business men, motoring along Loch Ness side yesterday forenoon, obtained an excellent view of the monster under perfect conditions. For once the creature moved slowly along the surface, with no great swirl of wash.

The men said that when 7½ miles east of Fort Augustus they saw the creature swimming about on the Glencoe side. It appeared to have been disturbed by the paddle steamer, Gondolier. Before it disappeared, the head, neck, and five distinct humps remained clearly in view for almost half hour.

The neck was eight feet long, and the body about thirty feet.

The men were Mr Andrew H. Robertson, manager, Messrs Roxburghe & Forrest, Rutland Square, Edinburgh; Mr W. Savage, of Messrs H. H. Alexander & Co., Semple Street, Edinburgh; and Mr Robert McGuire, plant engineer, Morton Quarry, near Edinburgh.

Aberdeen Journal - Wednesday 11 August 1937

MONSTER OUT AGAIN
PLUNGING ABOUT IN BORLUM BAY
SEEN FOR FIVE MINUTES

The Loch Ness monster has been making further appearances.

Its latest was in Borlum Bay, Fort-Augustus.

It was seen plunging about there on Monday night about 8.45 by Mrs Mary Ferguson, wife of the Rev. Donald Ferguson, minister of Fort-Augustus and Invermoriston Free Church, and her sister, Mrs K. Macdonald, 47 Stone Street, Newcastle-on-Tyne, who is on holiday at Fort-Augustus.

While returning along the Glencoe road, where they had gone for a walk, they noticed when, passing Borlum Farm, a tremendous upheaval in the waters of the loch below where they stood.

"A few minutes previously," said Mrs Ferguson, "we remarked that as the loch was so calm a view of the monster from such a fine vantage point would be worth seeing, and sure enough in a moment or two up the creature came.

"Three humps, a small one at either end and a much larger one in the middle, appeared and began to move slowly towards the middle of the bay, with a distinct undulating motion, and for more than five minutes we had a wonderful view of the strange animal.

"As it rolled about the disturbance in the water," Mrs Ferguson added, "was very pronounced, and we were surprised to see three seagulls fly towards the upheaval as though wondering what caused it, but, although the birds settled on the water, they kept at a distance from the humps."

Aberdeen Journal - Tuesday 17 August 1937

SCARE BY LOCH MONSTER
Appears Near Young Bathers

Another appearance by the Loch Ness monster comes to hand from Invermoriston.

There it gave a nasty scare to a party of young bathers enjoying a dip in the loch near the mouth of the river Moriston.

Scarcely had the party entered the water when Angus Stewart, the twelve-year-old son of Mr John Stewart, head gardener at Invermoriston Gardens, noticed what he described as "an ugly caterpillar-like thing" showing four or five humps coming towards the shore at a fast speed.

Shouting to the others, the boy at once made for the shore and, joined by the others, ran home.

On arrival there, Angus Stewart, with his two young sisters, was evidently distressed and became violently sick on telling his experience to his parents.

CARAVAN PARTY'S VIEW
MONSTER'S 15 SECONDS ON SURFACE

Six people have returned from their summer holiday to tell their friends all about the elusive monster of Loch Ness.

A Glasgow family and a Newcastle family spotted the monster giving a fifteen seconds display of surface evolutions at spot six miles beyond Invermoriston and opposite Foyers.

That was on the afternoon of August 3 but it was only yesterday that Mr W. H. Gibson, 88 Ardmay Crescent. King's Park, Glasgow, got back from his motor caravan tour of the Highlands to tell a "Press and Journal" representative of the encounter.

Mr Gibson was accompanied on his tour by his parents, Mr and Mrs Geo. Gibson. He explained that he had drawn his outfit into a quiet corner overlooking an inlet of the loch. His mother was looking out of the caravan window about 1.30 in the afternoon and Mr Gibson and his father were finishing lunch in the shade of the caravan.

They heard someone shout "There's something moving there." The call came from a party of three motorists drawn up nearby who proved to be Mr and Mrs F. Wood, and their daughter, Miss M. Wood, on a motoring tour from their home at Berwickhill Road, Ponteland. Newcastle.

"SOMETHING LIKE SEAL"

Mrs Gibson had a point of vantage and she immediately spotted a "longish necked creature something like a seal in colour." She saw the head "like a seal's, but smaller," but when Mr Gibson and his father ran round from the shade side of the caravan and looked over the water the monster was showing only humps.

"When got our eyes on the creature," said Mr Gibson, "she was about a hundred yards out, moving gracefully through the water. There was no splashing, but considerable wash was created. We saw the arch of a long neck and further back were two humps. The visibility was good and we had a grandstand view for fifteen seconds.

"The sun was shining brightly and brought out the colour of its skin, which was dark brown, like a seal. When first seen it was a hundred yards out and moved over the water for about fifty yards before submerging.

"It took a sudden dive, and the disturbance of the water showed that a creature of considerable bulk was moving swiftly along. Each hump would, I estimate, be about five feet long, and I consider that from the front part of the arched neck to the end of the last would be about fifteen feet. We could not detect any tail movement.

"VERY UNUSUAL"

"Only a matter of minutes before we spotted the creature my father had observed that if we had not seen the monster, at least we had had lunch at the spot where it had previously shown itself. Personally, I was a bit of a sceptic before, but now I am convinced that there is something very unusual in the loch.

"Other five people who think likewise are my parents and the Wood family. They were entire strangers to us, but when the monster disappeared they came running up and inquired if we had seen it.

"The six of us who saw the monster that day are convinced that it is neither a seal nor an overgrown porpoise, but definitely some strange specimen.

"We had cameras with us, but in the excitement of the moment forgot to get busy. In any case the sun was shining right across at us, and a snapshot with anything but a special camera would have been out of the question."

Yorkshire Evening Post - Wednesday 18 August 1937

LEEDS MAN SAW MONSTER
"Three Humps" in Loch Ness

A Leeds visitor to Loch Ness. Mr. J. Craigen, Harehills Place, Harehills Road, says he has seen the "monster."

He had been sceptical of statements made from time to time about the "monster," though as a native of the Inverness district he remembers that years ago parents threatened naughty children that they would be "thrown the beast Loch Ness."

"Sixty of us saw the monster," Mr. Craigen told a "Yorkshire Evening Post" reporter to-day. "I was on holiday with my sister and brother, and one night I went on a motor-coach tour to the Loch.

"By the loch side the driver shouted. There was crowd at that spot. I thought there had been an accident.

"We looked out over the Loch, and saw a head, part of a neck, and three humps. The head appeared to me about two feet long, rather like a crocodile's, but deeper.

"I reckon the neck was about six feet long, and the total length of the thing about 30 feet.

"It swam parallel to the shore, turned towards the shore and dived, and I didn't see it again. While it was visible it created quite awash, just as a motor-boat would."

Mr. Craigen said the time was shortly after eight in the evening.

"A shepherd there told us he had seen it often in many years," he said. "He also said that many other persons had seen it, but had not thought about it until it became famous.

Cave Theory

"Some people think that blasting during road work disturbed the monster from a cave in the loch. Loch Ness is reputed have caves beneath it.

"When I lived up there, I knew a boy who said had seen the monster. He called it a sea-horse, but I don't think any of us took much notice of his story."

Western Morning News - Wednesday 25 August 1937

'SEA SERPENT' AT WESTON
Monster Seen By Fisherman
HUMPS ON BACK AND SCALY TAIL

A "sea serpent" has been seen swimming off Weston-super-Mare.

A well-known local fisherman, Mr. Fred Hobbs, 75 George-street, Weston-super-Mare, yesterday described watching it for some little time on Monday morning.

He had taken some food for the seagulls at the rocks at Knightstone when suddenly he noticed the "monster" swimming towards the coast.

He exclaimed to the friend who was with him: "Look at that blessed great thing coming in with the tide."

Sixty feet from the shore there was a creature gliding forward, its head out of water, several humps on its back, and having a long tail covered with scales.

It was difficult to estimate its length in the water, Mr. Hobbs said, but he thought it was between 16 and 20 feet.

GLIDED SWIFTLY TO SEA.

It swam forward for a little way, then turned in the water, gliding swiftly out to sea against the flow of the tide.

"It put me in mind of the Loch Ness monster," said Mr. Hobbs, "and we watched for nearly half an hour until it was lost to sight in the Channel."

He and his friend then climbed the hill above Knightstone to see if they could follow the "serpent's" course from a greater height, but it had disappeared.

They did notice, however, a school of porpoises swimming out from the shore.

The weather was very clear at the time and the sea perfectly calm, so that it was possible to see for a long distance.

Nottingham Evening Post - Thursday 26 August 1937

A NEW "MONSTER" STORY.
"BIGGER AND BETTER THAN THAT OF LOCH NESS."
FISHERMEN DESCRIBE A "MERMAN."

The "monster" season has opened in Ireland - if the tale of two Connemara fishermen is to be believed.

A bigger and better "monster" than that of Loch Ness, it is claimed, has been discovered at Ballinakill Bay, near Renvyle, Connemara.

He is described as a "merman."

It is nearly nine months, according to the highest local authority, since he first made appearance. On that occasion, after creating a mild sensation, he retired to winter quarters. A few days ago he woke, and discovered it was summer. He also discovered that he was hungry, and cast his eye about for something to devour.

At this point two Connemara fishermen, Thomas O'Toole and Michael Ward, appeared on the scene in their curragh (a canvas-covered canoe).

The "merman," according to them, bobbed up beside the curragh. The fishermen at once made efforts to set up a new world's record for the flying half-mile with a curragh. The "merman" started in pursuit.

After a time, the story goes, the fishermen asked themselves why should they run away from a mere "merman"? Pulling in their oars they waited. Up came the "merman." The fishermen took stock of him.

He had, according to their version, straw-like, shaggy hair and beard, with very red lips and bushy eyebrows. His skin was fair in front and, by way of variety, blue on the back. He swam head and shoulders above the water.

When Ward threw him a mackerel he seized it eagerly, and dived under the water to consume it. In a few moments, according to the fishermen, he reappeared, smacking his lips and coming alongside the curragh with the evident intention of coming aboard. O'Toole decided that familiarity had gone too far, and gently chided the "merman" with an oar. The "monster" whinnied in pain and dived into the depths.

The fishermen made tracks for the shore, which they reached in safety, to tell their tale of adventure to the countryside.

Aberdeen Journal - Wednesday 22 September 1937

New proof of the Loch Ness Monster at Urquhart Castle. - A reptile's foot, 18 inches long, found on the shores of the loch. It has probably been shed by the monster after the manner of certain reptiles. The skin is hard and thick and the talons 4 inches long.

Dundee Courier - Tuesday 09 November 1937

Monster is Back from "Holiday"

After an absence of a month or so the Loch Ness monster has been clearly seen by a motoring party about four miles from Foyers.

Mr Peter Walker, B.Sc. (London), and his two sisters, Rosemary and Marguerite, the son and daughters of the Hon. Mrs Walker of Kingsmills, Inverness, were motoring along the south side of the loch when the ladies observed a large object over 50 yards from the shore.

There were humps on the "object," which seemed to be sunning itself. The motorists counted five humps before the monster set off at great speed.

Mr Walker said – "Neither the head nor tail could be seen, but I have no doubt it was the much-talked-of monster. It was a big one and a speedy one."

Aberdeen Journal - Tuesday 09 November 1937

LOCH NESS MONSTER
APPEARANCE FOUR MILES FROM FOYERS

The Loch Ness monster was clearly seen by a motoring party on Sunday afternoon about four miles from Foyers, on the south side of the loch.

Mr Peter Walker, B.Sc., London, and his two sisters, son and daughters of the Hon. Mrs Walker of Kingsmills, Inverness, were motoring along the lochside when they observed a large object basking in the water over fifty yards from the shore.

The loch was dead calm and the weather extraordinarily mild.

They distinctly counted five humps on the object, which after few minutes set off at a great speed, leaving a large trail on the water.

"There was no mistaking that the object was a big one and a speedy one, and," said Mr Walker, "we have no doubt that it was the monster."

Aberdeen Journal - Thursday 25 November 1937

MONSTER SEEN AGAIN WITHIN 50 YARDS OF SHORE BIG WASH MADE IN LOCH NESS

Mr A. W. S. Alexander, a retired officer of the Royal Engineers, who resides at Johnnie's Point, Invermoriston, had an excellent view of the Loch Ness monster while working at the loch side.

He told our representative that his attention was attracted by a heavy wash lapping the rocks on which he stood. This wash was caused by the monster as it raced past.

"There was no doubt about it," said Mr Alexander. "It was certainly the monster, in whose existence I have never believed, although I have fished the loch for salmon regularly during the past two years."

Mr Alexander stated that the so-called humps are undoubtedly caused by pronounced undulating motion, as the creature propels itself forward. Its speed, he stated, was from 25 to 30 miles per hour, and he thought the body extremely large - probably thirty to forty feet long.

The monster travelled parallel with the shore for about half-an-hour. and when passing the spot where Mr Alexander stood it was only fifty yards away. No head was visible, but the colour of the skin, which was silvery-grey, could be clearly seen in the bright sunshine. The loch at the time was flat and calm, and the waves caused by the creature continued to beat against the shore long after it had disappeared.

Yorkshire Evening Post - Tuesday 30 November 1937

Loch Monster of 1895

When, says the Duke of Portland, he first fished the River Garry and Loch Oich, in 1895, the fishermen often spoke of a horrible great beastie which they said appeared from time to time in Loch Ness.

"We ridiculed the reports, and chaffed them about the potency of the Fort Augustus whisky, but the proprietor of the Invergarry Hotel, who had been brought up at Invermoriston, assured me that his lather and he had actually seen the monster.

"I am glad to have an opportunity of making this statement, as it showed that the monster was known to exist more than 40 years ago. I for one fully believe its existence."

1938

Hull Daily Mail - Thursday 27 January 1938

Loch Ness Monster Back Again

The Loch Ness Monster, hibernating for the last two months, has appeared again, writes a London "Daily Mail" correspondent.

Father William McLellan, former parish priest of Glenfinnan, living in retirement at the Benedictine monastery at Fort Augustus, had an excellent view of the creature as it travelled along the calm surface of the loch towards Fort Augustus.

He said that while walking along the main Fort Augustus-Inverness road, he saw a high wash, which he thought was caused by a boat.

But in a few moments there appeared the monster's back, greyish, and broadly striped.

Local people declare that the monster has reappeared because of its fondness for flood water.

Aberdeen Journal - Thursday 27 January 1938

LOCH NESS MONSTER APPEARS AGAIN WATCHED BY PRIEST NEAR FORT-AUGUSTUS

After an interval of two months, the Loch Ness monster was seen again yesterday afternoon.

The Rev. Father William McLellan, a former parish priest of Glenfinnan, who has been living for the past year in retirement at St Benedict's Abbey, Fort-Augustus, had an excellent view of the creature as it travelled along the calm surface of the loch towards Fort-Augustus.

Father McLellan, in an interview, stated that he was taking his customary walk along the main Fort-Augustus-Inverness road, and when he reached a disused quarry at Portclair, about one and a quarter miles east of Fort- Augustus, he noticed a huge wash on the surface, speeding towards Fort-Augustus.

At first Father McLellan thought the wash had been caused by a boat, but in a few moments the monster's back appeared. It seemed to bear one or two broad stripes. The skin was of a greyish colour, but the monster was more or less enveloped in spray, so great was its speed.

After swimming for half mile on the surface, the monster plunged below but reappeared a second or two later, only to vanish again.

Two men working at drains on the Forestry Commission ground some time previously saw the monster travelling at a terrific speed. They estimated the length of its back at forty feet, and said it looked like an upturned boat.

Aberdeen Journal - Monday 07 February 1938

The "Mythical" Monster

Sir,- You report that Dr Henry Wood, when asked his opinion of the Loch Ness monster, replied that it is still a myth, as far as scientists are concerned. Must we therefore accept the conclusion that the famous monster has received his quietus?

Seeing is believing, and the large number of people who have seen it are surely entitled to believe in it.

Mr Mortimer Batten was asked the same question after a lecture which he recently delivered, and he replied that he was quite sure of its existence. He said that in the year 1914 some people fishing from a boat on the loch got the fright of their lives when a monster with three humps suddenly appeared quite near the boat, and proceeded up the loch at a terrific pace, and, to quote his words, "that was long before the Loch Ness monster became newspaper stunt."

Each generation of scientists seem to spend a considerable proportion of their time and energy in proving that their predecessors were wrong in most of their opinions, so there is still hope that some day the existence of the monster will be scientifically established - Humpyosaurus.

Aberdeen Journal - Tuesday 01 March 1938

MONSTER OF LOCH NESS
WATCHED FROM BOAT AND SHORE
"90 FEET LONG," SAYS OBSERVER

The Loch Ness monster has been seen again, and excellent views of the creature were described by men from Foyers and Invermoriston.

Two Foyers men who had been out salmon fishing on the loch said that between nine and ten o'clock in the morning they were rowing towards the half-way house when the monster appeared about twenty yards away, showing between six and eight feet of its back above water. It cruised around on the surface quietly for a quarter of an hour, and finally submerged in the direction of Invermoriston.

One of the men wanted to row the boat closer, but his companion said he had seen all he wished to convince him that the loch harbours a very large and very strange creature.

Five hours later, Mr Donald MacDonald, mail contractor, Invermoriston, saw what he described as a staggering sight, while he was tending his ship on a hill overlooking his house.

"I glanced at the loch," he said, "and there was the monster, quite close to the mouth of the River Moriston, and diving every few moments.

"I know that people will laugh," Mr MacDonald proceeded, "when I say that this fish or animal was fully ninety feet long. At first I thought it must be a barge floating upside down, but although I could scarcely believe my eyes I am certain I am giving an honest estimation of its length."

Mr MacDonald watched the monster for six minutes, then it dived below with a considerable commotion. It was heading towards Foyers.

Aberdeen Journal - Thursday 21 April 1938

LOCH NESS MONSTER SEEN BY FORT WILLIAM RECTOR

The Loch Ness monster was seen on Tuesday by the Rev. Leslie Rule Wilson, rector of St Andrew's Episcopal Church, Fort-William, and three Edinburgh friends - Mr Alister Erskine Murry, Mr Alexander Goodall, and Mr John Franckeiss.

"We were returning to Fort-William by car from Glen Affric," Mr Wilson said in an interview last night. "As we were passing a point on the road high up above the loch near the Halfway House between Urquhart Castle and

Fort-Augustus, Mr Franckeiss, who was sitting at the back, shouted out 'There's something in the water.'

SIX BLACK HUMPS

"Near the middle of the loch we saw six black humps, each sticking about four feet out of the water. I should say the animal would be about forty feet in length, and that the humps were not due to the movement of the creature, but were part of its structure."

"It played about in the water for about five minutes, setting up a terrific commotion like boiling water on the otherwise calm surface. Then it moved forward and gradually sank out of sight.

"I was almost as much impressed by the huge wash which swept the beach about two minutes after it disappeared as I was by the monster itself, regarding the existence of which I had been very sceptical up till now."

Mr Erskine Murry said: "The creature is like nothing I've ever seen before. It gave an impression of immense solidity with its six massive humps."

Yorkshire Evening Post - Monday 09 May 1938

ENTER THE MONSTER

The following appears in "The Times" above the signature of C. B. Prickett, Rear-Admiral, Glastullich, Nigg Station, Rossshlre:-

On April 25, at two o'clock in the afternoon, my wife and I were looking out over Loch Ness from the Halfway House Hotel, Invermortston. The weather was fine and clear, but a light westerly breeze raised a good ripple on the water.

About 200 yards from us and moving slowly from west to east we saw a dark rounded hump break the surface and dive. It was followed immediately by another the same size, perhaps 10 ft behind it.

I would have said that I had seen two large porpoises, but there is no sea water within 20 miles, and, unlike porpoises, these objects did not reappear, although we waited hopefully for about half an hour.

Hartlepool Mail - Monday 16 May 1938

Writes a "Times" correspondent: A scheme is now in formation to try to establish the identity of the Loch Ness monster. If a strange animal had been reported as having made its appearance in the wilds of Central Asia or Africa, expeditions would have long ago started out to prove its existence; but though the presence of something out of the ordinary has been reported by hundreds of people in a loch at our own doors no serious attempt to solve the mystery has been made. From a scientific point of view it is extremely important that steps with this object in view should be taken.

Dundee Courier - Wednesday 18 May 1938

Out For The Monster

A naval officer is the latest person who has decided to disturb the peace of the Loch Ness monster.

He is Captain Donald John Munro, of New Galloway, and he means to form a company to hunt the monster.

To a reporter yesterday he said – "I mean to use the latest scientific equipment in this attempt. I will use sounding gear and range finders.

"Submarines are not feasible. We must take the utmost care not to disturb it in any way.

"The monster has been wallowing in Loch Ness for five years now. It is about time he was caught."

Portsmouth Evening News - Tuesday 24 May 1938

A SEA MONSTER!
PORTSMOUTH ANGLER SEES ONE AT SPITHEAD

Southsea is at last coming into line with other popular seaside resorts, such as Loch Ness. Monsters have been the vogue for years in Scotland, and a merman was seen off the Irish Coast by some fishermen last summer; but the South Coast has rather lagged behind in this respect.

But now, the summer sea serpent's season having opened, Portsmouth is well in the forefront with a five-humped 35-foot monster!

Mr. William Oastler, who is an engineer at the Gordon Sanitary Laundry, saw it. He was fishing with some friends two miles off the Spit Buoy, when he was suddenly confronted with this latest addition to the monster history of the South Coast.

In an interview, he said:- "It was a funny looking object, with about four or five humps and about 35 feet long. We were anchored when we first saw it, and I was a bit windy, as I am not a very good swimmer, and did not know what might happen if it got under the boat, but it was heading fast for the Isle of Wight."

Mr. Oastler and his two friends had seen sufficient of porpoises to be certain they were not confusing the monster with them. He described it as being of a silvery grey colour, with its humps standing four or five feet out of the water.

Hartlepool Mail - Tuesday 07 June 1938

THE MONSTER
SEEING IT "NO LONGER NEWS"

Lt. Colonel Guy Liddel writes to the "Times" as follows; As there are still some unbelievers about, may I assist in sweeping away the cobwebs of doubt?

In September, 1934, I was in a Scottish youth hostel near Port Augustus, and its warden was Mrs. Cameron, who lived in an adjacent cottage She has lived all her life within a mile or two of Loch Ness.

In 1919. when she was a girl of 15, she and her two young brothers were spending a sunny September afternoon on the Loch side quite close to the boathouse of Inchnacardoch House, about six furlongs from Fort Augustus. The loch at this point shallows, forming a narrow bay with a marshy peninsula on the north side of which a ruined steam launch is stranded.

As the children were playing on the strand they saw the monster on the shore of the marsh opposite, lurching down to the water, "humping its shoulders and twisting its head from side to side."

"WALKED LIKE AN ELEPHANT"

Mrs Cameron said it walked like an elephant. I asked her what the back looked like. She said they did not wait to see, as the bairns were terrified and never stopped running till they reached home. They were scolded by their parents who told them that "Old Nick was after them for gathering nuts on the Sabbath." Mrs. Cameron saw the monster again in July, 1934, when returning from Inverness by motor-bus, and so did all the passengers.

The monster seems to have a predilection for the north side of the Loch from Drumnadrochit to Inchnacardoch, and the deepest water is found there. The magnificent new road from Inverness to Fort Augustus runs high above the water on the rocky hillside. The constant blasting during its construction caused the saurian much uneasiness, and it was much more seen on the surface in those days. The road was finished four years ago. Seeing the monster is no longer news In Port Augustus.

Dundee Evening Telegraph - Saturday 11 June 1938

Probing the Secret of Loch Ness

Captain D. J. Munro, R.N. (Ret.), Clearwell, New Galloway, has issued a pamphlet with his proposals for a scheme to determine the nature of the Loch Ness monster.

He places out of bounds for this purpose all plans based on aeroplanes, bathospheres, and submarines as being unsuitable. To observe it successfully perfect quietness in water and air is essential; this can only be secured by observing from fixed stations ashore and afloat.

There is, he says, no use running about the lochside with portable cameras or other instruments of precision, or travelling on the surface of the loch in motor boats. Fixed stations, with observers and instruments always ready for action, will be the only possible means of securing satisfactory results.

He proposes three fixed stations, each in a position to be seen from the other. Each station would be fitted with a telephoto camera, a range-finder, a cinema camera with lens for long-range work, and other equipment. He estimates the cost of carrying on operations with suitable observers at £500 for each station for a period of three months.

For each station he proposes one naval officer in charge of a trained observer, one marine or bluejacket, and two others who might be volunteers.

Very Timid.

Each station would have one observer on watch from daylight to twilight, and at least two others always ready to man the instruments if the creature was sighted. To finance the scheme, he suggests the formation of a company with one shilling shares.

In the course of his notes Captain Munro states of the creature that undoubtedly it is very timid, and dives immediately any strange noise is heard, such as a motor horn or propeller of a motor boat.

"Having made five voyages in clipper ships round the world," he writes, "I have seen more life in the sea in one voyage than in 45 years in steamships. Fish of all descriptions, and animals such as whales, are afraid of the vibrations set up by propellers."

Like all wild creatures, it is more than probable that early morning is the time of day when it frequents the surface. Then the loch is not disturbed by motor boats, and the roads are also quieter; but this is just the time of day when there are few people about.

So many people, Captain Munro asserts, have now seen and reported its appearance that their observations cannot be put down to romancing, defective vision, or hysteria.

Hartlepool Mail - Tuesday 14 June 1938

The "Monster"

If sufficient money is forthcoming, we are likely to get a solution to the Loch Ness mystery. Capt. D. J. Munro. RN. (retired), who went to sea at the age of 11 years, and who has been round the world five times, is forming a limited liability company, with one shilling shares, to enable a scientific investigation to be made into the habits, appearance. and likes and dislikes of the famous "monster." Captain Munro has written a pamphlet on the subject, and he says £1,500 would be necessary to carry on operations for three months. It must be understood, he writes, that "no dividends can be expected." At the same time, if good "shots" are obtained by the cameras, the results may be valuable and recoup the subscribers, and perhaps something more. Captain Munro thinks if a silhouette could be taken from a position on the same plane as the "monster," and its length, speed of its travel, and the nature of its food ascertained, reasonable interest would be satisfied.

Capt. Munro is puzzled by the source of the food which an animal of the size of the "monster" must consume. Trout, pike, salmon, and eels are known to be in the loch, but trout would be the only all-the-year-round food supply, "and a creature of the size described must be very nimble to be able to make a meal of them. There are no large masses of rushes or grass on the banks of the loch to give it a vegetable diet; and the trees do not show any signs of being attacked. ... In the deeper parts of the loch there may be an unknown food supply; and this could only be found by suitable trawling gear."

Aberdeen Journal - Thursday 30 June 1938

SAW MONSTER AT 20 YARDS
GLENURQUART MAN ASTONISHED
TAIL FULLY SIX FEET LONG

A Glenurquhart man, Mr John McLean, had a close view of the Loch Ness monster about a quarter-past nine o'clock on Tuesday night.

He was standing at the shore near the mouth of the Altsigh Burn watching whether any trout were rising, as he thought of going fishing, when he saw what he describes as "an extraordinary sight."

"It was the monster's head and neck less than twenty yards from me," he said, "and it was, without any doubt, in the act of swallowing food. It opened and closed its mouth several times quite quickly, and then kept tossing its head backwards in exactly the same manner as a cormorant does after it has devoured a fish."

What the monster had eaten, Mr McLean could not say, but he thought a trout of from one to two pounds in weight would be as much as it could manage at a time.

He also said that at that particular spot the water teems with excellent trout.

TWO HUMPS

No sooner had the creature finished its meal than it dived below, but before doing so two distinct humps and the entire length of the tail came to the surface.

The monster then vanished head first, but came up again a few yards further west, and there it lay for two or three minutes on the top of the water.

The tail was again quite clear at the surface, with the head, neck, and two humps showing. In a moment or two it began to dive very slowly and, in doing so, the head was submerged first, followed by the humps, but at this point the foremost hump became very much larger and rose in fact almost twice as high out of the water as it had been at any time during its appearance.

18 TO 22 FEET LONG

Summing up his description of the creature, Mr Maclean said: "I was absolutely petrified with astonishment, and if I did have a camera with me I was so excited that I would probably have spoiled the chance of a lifetime.

"The monster, I am sure, is eighteen to twenty-two feet long, the tail fully six feet, and the largest hump was about three feet high. The head is small and pointed, the skin very dark brown on the back, and like that of a horse when wet and glistening. The neck is rather thin and several feet long, but I saw no flippers or fins."

This, it may be added, is the first time that anyone has seen the monster full length above water or out of it, and the entire tail, which was about a foot thick at the root and tapered to a fine point.

Dundee Evening Telegraph - Tuesday 19 July 1938

SAW LOCH NESS MONSTER
"Huge, Dark Object"

Two Bankfoot men, Mr J. Allison, Church Lane, and Mr James Robertson, Main Street, motoring round Loch Ness were fortunate enough to see the monster.

Mr Allison, in an interview, explained that although the monster was some distance out it was easily discernible from the road.

Eagerly scanning the water for miles in the hope of glimpsing the monster, they were at last rewarded when they espied a huge dark object moving over the surface of the water, with one fin showing distinctly.

Unfortunately their view was of short duration, but sufficient to assure them that they had seen the much-talked-of monster.

Hartlepool Mail - Saturday 30 July 1938

STRONG MEN TO HUNT MONSTER
NIGHT AND DAY VIGIL AT LOCH NESS

An organised effort is to be made in the last two weeks of August to capture the Loch Ness monster.

Mr Peter Kent, a young man associated with a London theatre, and Miss Marion Sperling who assists him, have planned to spend two weeks on the edge of the loch keeping watch day and night.

They are taking with them 12 strong men for whom they advertised. The party will be armed with a system of nets and the latest high-powered whaling gun.

The 12 strong men were wanted to man the camps some half-a-dozen of which are to be set up on the waterside, and assist in the attempt to capture the "beastie," dead or alive.

"It may sound rather fantastic," Mr. Kent said in an interview, "but we are convinced there is a creature of considerable interest in the loch.

"It may be nothing more than a fish about 20ft long with a large head, but no one has properly organized a search, and we think if there is something there it will be of considerable scientific interest.

"We feel it may come to man power, in which case we shall be at an advantage with a body of strong men at hand.

"We are going up at this time because it is at this time of the year that the 'monster' is supposed to appear."

Aberdeen Journal - Wednesday 03 August 1938

LOCH MONSTER AGAIN SEEN BY INVERNESS LORRY DRIVER

The Loch Ness monster made another appearance yesterday forenoon.

It was seen by Mr James Forsyth, a motor lorry driver employed by Mr Charles Ross, Midmills Garage, Inverness.

Mr Forsyth, who lives at 49 Kessock Avenue, Inverness, was loading gravel near the stone-crushing plant at Lochend when a lad who was assisting him drew his attention to a black shape rising out of the water about 150 yards from the shore.

"The two humps," Mr Forsyth told a "Press and Journal" representative, "looked exactly like two large barrels. I expected to see the monster's head rise out of the water, but only the two humps appeared, and, after remaining stationary for a few seconds, the monster suddenly shot across the Loch for about a hundred yards at a speed of about twenty-five miles per hour.

"Shortly after that," Mr Forsyth said, "the monster went under the surface. Its skin seemed to be rough and leathery, and although I did not believe in the monster's existence before, my experience has convinced me that the story is no myth."

Aberdeen Journal - Tuesday 09 August 1938

LOCH MONSTER BROADCAST PROGRAMME TO BE GIVEN ON AUGUST 21

The Loch Ness Monster has been a popular news item for almost five years.

Soon it will be still further blazoned on the annals of history.

The British Broadcasting Corporation are out to immortalise the beast, and on August 21, listeners to a programme to be broadcast from Edinburgh will have the opportunity to decide for themselves whether the evidence produced in favour of the Monster's existence is worthy of acceptance.

FOUR-DAY TOUR

For four days a B.B.C. recording van toured the Loch Ness district in search of facts and witnesses, under the direction of Mr John Pudney, specially sent from London, who was in charge of the research work, and is acting as producer of the finished programme.

Already the B.B.C. has attempted to plumb some puzzling mysteries of long standing in their series "Fact or Fiction." Unicorns, mermaids and the lost continent of Atlantis are among the subjects which have been discussed, and now the Monster will come under the all-seeing eye.

FOR AND AGAINST

Among witnesses for the "Defence" - those who claim to have seen the Monster - are a monk from the Fort Augustus Monastery, two lorry drivers, a garage proprietor, and a schoolboy.

For the "Prosecution" is Dr E. G. Boulenger, director of the London Zoo's aquarium, an authority on water life, who will argue against the possibility of the Monster's existence.

Aberdeen Journal - Wednesday 10 August 1938

HALF-HOUR VIEW OF MONSTER MOTORISTS IN LUCK AT LOCH NESS

Over forty people are believed to have seen the Loch Ness monster near Drumnadrochit yesterday.

Motorists in the vicinity of the village on the north side of the loch saw the monster disporting itself for nearly half an hour.

It appeared at first like a dark mark on the loch, but gradually, as it approached nearer the observers distinguished a hump on the back of the black body.

One of the party of motorists who watched the monster was Mr A. Mackenzie, Culcabock, Inverness, who was accompanied by Mr A. O. Maclaren.

He said he saw the monster first at 2.15 in the afternoon, and watched it for just under half an hour.

The monster, he said, was more than half a mile from the shore, but they could distinguish its black body with a large hump on the back. The monster moved slowly away, and after travelling about 200 yards it gradually disappeared.

Mr Mackenzie added that more than twelve cars were at the roadside, and the occupants saw the monster. Some of the occupants of the car had binoculars, and were able to get a much better view than he had.

Dundee Courier - Wednesday 10 August 1938

Loch Ness Monster Seen Again But German Naval Visitors Missed It

Mr A. Maclaren, Inverness, a press photographer, saw the Loch Ness monster near Drumnadrochit yesterday. Although equipped with his camera, he was unable to get a photograph, as the monster was about half mile away.

Mr Maclaren was accompanied by Mr Alex. Mackenzie, an Inverness reporter, and they state that the monster was moving in the direction of Fort Augustus.

They could see its head and part of its back above the water, and they estimated its length at about ten feet.

"It was futile," said Mr Maclaren, "to attempt to get a photograph. It would only come out as a black speck. I would have required a telescopic lens."

Shortly after Mr Maclaren had seen the monster, Provost Hugh Mackenzie and a party of visiting German naval officers motored along, but by this time the monster had disappeared. The German sailors were naturally disappointed.

Aberdeen Journal - Saturday 13 August 1938

MOVE TO BAN HUNT FOR MONSTER TRAWLER WITH WHALING GUN AND NETS

The arrival at Fort Augustus of Mr Peter Kent and Miss Stirling, who have come from London prepared to spend £5000 in an effort to capture the Loch Ness monster, has caused considerable interest in the district, and local people view the project with disapproval

It is understood that a trawler equipped with a whaling gun and special nets will be used, and that those taking part in the hunt will include explorers and men who have hunted whales.

Several local men who are closely connected with public administration have already received requests from various places calling upon them to use their influence to have the monster hunt banned.

Mr R. McBean Fraser, who represents Fort Augustus on Inverness County Council, stated in an interview that, so far as he could see, the monster hunters stand very little chance of success owing to the loch having an average depth of over 600 feet.

At the same time he considered that steps should be taken to prevent anyone destroying the monster, which he has himself seen on several occasions in the past few years.

Meanwhile the monster has put in another appearance near the Fort Augustus end of the loch, where it was watched by a squad of workmen employed by Messrs A. M. Carmichael, Edinburgh, on the reconstruction of the Glencoe-Whitebridge Road.

Dundee Courier - Saturday 13 August 1938

THE THREAT TO THE MONSTER

Somebody said long ago that if an archangel were to make its appearance in this country quite an appreciable number of the inhabitants would at once get after it with a gun.

We must have improved a good deal since the pronouncement of this dictum, for the Loch Ness monster (not, to be sure, an archangel, but sharing with it the qualities of strangeness and unfamiliarity that excite the shooting instinct) has now been an object of lively interest for some years and nobody has planned its destruction.

That, however, could not last, and in recent days paragraphs have appeared in the papers telling us that certain persons are planning to equip a vessel with whale-hunting weapons and proceed to the killing or capture of the interesting creature.

Probably few believed it. In what old-fashioned journalists used to call the silly season that kind of paragraph tends to get written and launched in the flagging news stream.

But to-day we are told that the misguided adventurers have actually arrived at Fort-Augustus prepared to make good their menace, and that there is a strong and indignant local reaction.

That local reaction will, we are sure, have wide and sympathetic backing.

Why should the monster be hunted down? Of all the thrill producers of this thrill-craving age it is surely the most innocuous; one might put higher and say the most beneficent.

In the legends of past times the monsters which haunted Highland lochs and rivers - kelpies and suchlike - acquired a grim and ghastly reputation. They lay in wait for wayfarers and carried them to a watery doom.

But the Loch Ness monster has for years lived a consistent and blameless life. Not even a Presbytery of the Free Presbyterians has found cause to inveigh against it, from which it is a fair inference that it never makes its appearance Sundays.

In its perfect and complete harmlessness it presents an inspiring example to the inhabitants of this or any other land. There is multiplied testimony that never has it done more than exhibit itself and communicate its thrill.

Sometimes it is more thrilling than at others. It has been known to lie like a log and do nothing at all. In more sportive mood it rears up its giraffe-like neck and surveys the fascinating landscape of Glen Albyn. At its very best it manifests its far-famed humps and displays its notable turn of speed.

But never on any occasion has it gone beyond registering a thrill.

But its excellence is not merely negative. Perhaps without design on its part it has accomplished more than any other known agency in the way of improving the tourist industry of the Northern Highlands. Hundreds, probably thousands, of people have gone there to be thrilled. Many have been disappointed. But hope springs eternal in the human breast, and most of them will go there again. And that is all to the good of the Highlands.

Perhaps considerations of this kind are moving the inhabitants of the lochside who are now protesting against the plans of the would-be hunters, not less than their natural Highland sympathy with the mysterious. But that is nothing to their discredit in an age which never blushes to find itself harbouring thoughts of material advantage.

It all amounts to this, that the monster is a good thing, and why should a good thing be hunted down?

That is a ticklish question to answer, and one can only guess how the hunters would answer it.

Probably they would profess a scientific curiosity. Probably the man with a gun who took a pot-shot at an archangel would make the same profession. It is the pretext of all the misfortunes who cannot see a live rare bird or beast without wishing to see it dead and stuffed. For our part, we do not believe in that scientific curiosity, and join with Fort-Augustus in saying "Hands off our monster."

There is, of course, the high likelihood that it is superfluous to do anything about it.

The monster has a remarkable faculty for looking after itself. It hardly ever appears when it is looked for. Thousands have gone out with cameras to take its picture, and, except on the rarest occasions, it has made its appearances when all the cameras were elsewhere.

Loch Ness is about twenty miles in length and, as we are reminded to-day, 600 feet in depth. It is an ideal home for a monster which loves privacy except at the rare moments when it is moved to impart a thrill. Unlike a whale or porpoise, it appears to be under no necessity to come to the surface to "blow." Therefore it has almost limitless power of avoiding imnertinent curiosity.

It is a hundred to one that the trawler or harpooner who goes after it will get nothing but wet water and fresh air for his pains.

All the same the misguided enterprise should be vigorously interdicted. A monster of the highest character, like this one, ought not to be molested, especially by destructive-minded aliens. Can the Ness Fishery Board not warn them off the ground? It seems to be one of the occasions when one could do with a dictator.

Dundee Courier - Monday 15 August 1938

Monster Hunters Warned Off

The statement that there is to be a hunt by a trawler for the Loch Ness monster and that an effort will be made to harpoon the creature is not taken too seriously by the police.

At the same time, they are taking no chances, and have made it known in Inverness and Loch Ness-side that every precaution will be taken to prevent any person interfering with the creature.

Proprietors of land marching the loch will also have a say in any scheme likely to interfere in the angling, which goes on daily.

The idea of a trawler hunting with harpoons is looked upon as fanciful, not only from the fact that the Caledonian Canal authorities would have some say in it sailing into Loch Ness, but also in view of the great length of the loch.

Aberdeen Journal - Tuesday 16 August 1938

ON TRAIL OF MONSTER
PREPARATIONS BY EXPEDITION
LOCH NESS HUNT AT WEEK-END

It is reported that a start will be made next week-end in the big hunt for the Loch Ness monster.

The party have returned to London, and it is stated that when they come North again they will be accompanied by more than twenty strong men as assistants.

The equipment will include a thirty-five-feet-long steel tank in which the monster will be placed if it is captured, a fast speed-boat armed with a harpoon gun, an outsize in trawl nets bound with steel hawsers, and modern photographic equipment.

As the result of a visit paid to Loch Ness during the past week-end, it has been decided to make Fort-Augustus the headquarters of the expedition, and between there and Invermoriston observing stations equipped with short-wave wireless transmitting sets will be established.

Immediately any of the observers sight the monster, word will be sent to Fort-Augustus and the leaders will leave in a speed-boat in an effort to capture the monster.

Already the leaders of the expedition, who have seen the monster twice since coming North, have been warned by the police that the monster must not harmed.

In the Fort-Augustus and Invermoriston districts the general opinion is that the present attempt will be no more successful than previous hunts for the monster.

Dundee Courier - Wednesday 17 August 1938

Monster Heads For Priests' Boat

The Loch Ness monster was seen by two priests on holiday at Fort-Augustus, who were out in a rowing boat yesterday - Father M. McKinnon, Island of Barra, and Father Grimes, Liverpool.

They said they first noticed the monster's back, about 10 feet long and three or four feet above water, slightly east of Glendoe boathouse. They rowed closer, and the creature made off towards the Invermoriston shore.

Father McKinnon said the tail was clearly seen about 20 feet behind the hump, but the head never appeared.

The monster than turned and came toward the boat. When it was 50 yards off Father Grimes decided to make for the shore.

Just then the pleasure steamer Gondolier came along, and after it had passed there was no sign of the monster. Altogether the priests watched it for over an hour.

Dundee Courier - Monday 22 August 1938

M.P. URGES STATE MUST SAVE MONSTER

Following the report that a party from London will endeavour to capture or harpoon the Loch Ness monster, Sir Murdoch Macdonald, M.P., who is holidaying in Inverness, has written to the Secretary for Scotland asking that immediate steps be taken to prevent any action that might endanger the monster's life.

He asks that the police be given instructions to see that nothing is left undone to prevent what would be nothing less than an unwarranted piece of vandalism.

Sir Murdoch points out that five years ago he wrote Sir Godfrey Collins, then Secretary for Scotland, asking that the police be instructed to see that no persons be allowed to interfere with the monster. Sir Godfrey replied that he had been in communication with the Chief Constable of Inverness-shire, who had stated that he would take steps to warn residents and as many visitors as possible that nothing must be done to endanger the life of the creature.

Sir Murdoch adds that he sees no reason why the police should not act in the matter, but if nothing can be done he would, as he had said before, ask that a short Bill be brought in for the safeguarding of the monster. There was a precedent for that in the famous case of Pelorus Jack (a whale which was specially protected by the New Zealand Government).

Aberdeen Journal - Friday 26 August 1938

TOURISTS SEE MONSTER
SEEMED ABOUT FIFTEEN FEET LONG

The Loch Ness monster was seen by a party of tourists from the balcony of the Half-Way House, near Invermoriston, shortly after lunch time yesterday.

They had an excellent view of the creature.

The witnesses included visitors from London and Stafford, also Miss Peggy Maclennan, Achnasheen, Ross-shire, and Miss Fraser, proprietrix of the hotel.

The sunshine and calm water made observation perfect.

First the head came up, then two humps and lastly the tail, which in the words of Miss Maclennan, "Shot out of the water."

It lay basking for four minutes, then with a considerable wash from the tail disappeared.

Soon afterwards it came up again much closer to the shore and continued swimming at a fair speed towards the Urquhart Castle side.

None of the witnesses had a camera.

The total length the creature seemed to be fifteen feet and the colour dark brown, shading to a much lighter tone on the underparts.

The visitors were delighted to have seen the monster.

Dundee Courier - Monday 29 August 1938

20 Strong Men Booked to Hunt Monster This Week
Speed Boat Chartered

It was learned at the week-end that Mr Peter Kent and Miss Stirling, who were recently at Loch Ness with the object of arranging a large-scale hunt for the capture, dead or alive, of the monster, are definitely to make the attempt this week.

They are coming with 20 strong men from London, and it is understood that a speedboat, which will carry a harpoon gun, has been chartered at Inverness.

Some of the men will operate from Fort Augustus and the others will be posted further down the loch.

The people of the district are not the only ones to protest. Within the past few days Mr W. U. Goodbody, Invergarry, a member of Inverness County Council, has received letters from as far away as Holland, asking him to do all in his power to defeat what one correspondent called "this nefarious scheme."

More letters, including one from Dorset, have been addressed to Mr McBean Fraser, who represents Fort Augustus on the County Council.

The promoters are stated to be prepared to spend £5000 on the venture, and while their chances of success are admittedly small, one lucky hit with the exploding harpoon would mean the end of a creature that is as mysterious as it is famous.

Dundee Courier - Wednesday 31 August 1938

Monster Races Tug
SEVEN HUMPS THIS TIME

The steam tug Arrow, on her maiden voyage from Leith to Manchester, had a distinguished escort on Loch Ness - the monster.

Captain and crew were exceptionally favoured, for the creature showed no fewer than seven humps. A special entry was made in the ship's log.

Two and half miles east of Urquhart Castle, said Captain Brodie, Leith, in an interview, he noticed "a huge black-coloured animal, rather like a hump-backed whale," emerge and keep pace with the ship. It showed two humps.

All the crew except a fireman came on deck to watch.

The monster dived, but in a few moments reappeared. This time it showed seven humps or coils, and tore past the tug at terrific speed just on the surface.

LIKE GIANT SERPENT.

The coils, according to P. Byrne, Leith, deckhand, reminded him of a giant serpent, glistening in the sunshine. The loch was almost calm, but the disturbance set up by the monster was amazing, said Captain Brodie.

Mr Rich, the mate, said he had never in all his seafaring experience seen anything like it. He thought the length of the two humps first seen was fully 15 feet, and as it raced past the ship only a short distance away, with seven humps showing, Captain Brodie estimated it was at least half as long as the tug, this being between 30 and 40 feet.

Previously he had been sceptical about the monster. Now he is convinced.

Aberdeen Journal - Wednesday 31 August 1938

"ASTOUNDED" CREW
LOCH NESS MONSTER SEEN TWICE
HALF AS LONG AS TUG

An unusually fine view of the Loch Ness monster was had by the captain, mate and the crew of the steam tug Arrow.

The tug, which is owned by the Manchester Canal authorities, was on her maiden voyage from Leith to Manchester.

Its appearance amazed those on board the tug.

"When passing up Loch Ness, two miles and a half east of Urquhart Castle," said Captain Brodie, Leith, in an interview, "the mate, Mr Rich, also from Leith, and myself noticed a huge black-coloured animal rather like a hump-backed whale emerge on the loch's surface and keep pace with the ship for some distance.

HUGE CREATURE

"We at once realised it was the monster. We were honestly astounded at seeing such a huge creature in an inland loch, but, believe me," said Captain Brodie, "this was no whale, because just behind the foremost hump was another, and no whale ever had two distinct humps. By this time all the crew except a fireman had rushed on deck to see the monster, but only in time to watch it dive below."

In a few moments it re-appeared, and, in the captain's own words, the appearance was "even more astonishing" than the first; as the creature now showed seven humps or coils, and tore past the tug at a terrific speed just on the surface.

LIKE GIANT SERPENT

The coils, according to P. Myrne, Leith, a deckhand, reminded him of a giant serpent glistening brightly in the sunshine. The loch was almost calm, but the wash set up by the monster was amazing, said Captain Brodie.

Mr Rich, the mate, said he had never in all his seafaring experiences seen anything like it.

He estimated the length of the two humps first seen at fully fifteen feet, but as to the creature's length, as it raced past the ship only a short distance away with seven humps showing, Captain Brodie and his son, William, said it was at least half as long as the tug, this being somewhere between thirty and forty feet.

Captain Brodie said he was so impressed by what he saw that he made a special entry of the incident in the ship's log.

Previously, he stated, he had been very sceptical about the monster, out now he realises that Loch Ness does contain an animal that tallies with no known sea creature.

Other members of the crew who witnessed the appearances were Chief Engineer Sprunt and Donald Campbell, both of Glasgow, and Wm. Lamb and P. Byrne, Leith.

Portsmouth Evening News - Wednesday 31 August 1938

LOCH NESS
Here's That Monster Again

The skipper and crew of the steam tug Arrow, passing through Loch Ness yesterday state that they saw "the monster" close at hand off Castle Urquhart, one and a half miles from Drumnadrochit, Inverness-shire.

The Arrow was steaming at more than ten knots, yet the monster, they say, passed her like a streak, setting up a wash which rocked the tug.

Capt. William Brodie, of Leith, the skipper, before leaving Fort Augustus, Inverness-shire, said: "I never believed the tales I heard, but when I saw this creature I realized that it was monster. I was astounded by its size.

"It was black and rather like a humped whale. But it was no whale, I have seen dozens of them."

Aberdeen Journal - Friday 02 September 1938

MONSTER AGAIN SEEN
TWO APPEARANCES IN HALF-HOUR
BACK EIGHT TO TEN FEET LONG

Within half-an-hour the Loch Ness monster made two appearances near Invermoriston and was seen by nine persons.

It was first observed about ten o'clock in the forenoon.

At that time Mr William Grant, mail driver, Invermoriston, and several other men saw the monster indulging in a shower bath just off Invermoriston pier, throwing up the water with terrific force and moving slowly westward.

Thirty minutes later a man who has lived on Loch Ness-side for the past eighteen years, and had never seen it before and who did not believe in its existence, had, in his own words, "the last doubt removed."

He is Mr James McEwan, head forester with the Scottish Forestry Commission at Portclair.

He stated that the monster's back came to the surface very quietly slightly west of the forestry nursery.

"It was," he said, "so like an upturned boat that I called to three of our men, Messrs George and Alfred Ross and

Gordon Mackenzie, 'There's a canoe,' but suddenly the 'canoe' became very much alive, and without any warning plunged below."

Mr McEwan said the monster's back was eight to ten feet long, two feet high and of a distinct brown colour.

Gloucestershire Echo - Thursday 08 September 1938

LOCH NESS MONSTER SEEN AGAIN
Cotswold Visitors Have A Clear View

The Loch Ness "Monster" was on Tuesday seen by Capt. de Winton, of Tally Ho!, Andoversford, and his sister-in-law, Mrs. Grice-Hutchinson, so clearly as to give considerable weight to the evidence that the monster is what it is claimed to be.

Capt. de Winton and Mrs. Grice-Hutchinson, and other members of the family, are at Whitebridge, Inverness, for the shooting.

A Scottish correspondent in a letter to the editor of the "Echo" writes:-

"Captain de Winton, accompanied by Mrs. Grice-Hutchinson, was proceeding to Whitebridge, by way of Loch Ness, when he saw, just below Castle Urquhart, what was undoubtedly the Loch Ness Monster.

"Both Captain de Winton and Mrs. Grice-Hutchinson had a good view of the monster, which was proceeding quickly through the water, and showed several humpish lumps towards the tail end.

"From their estimates the monster is about 30 to 40 feet in length.

"Another car with two Scottish gentlemen also stopped and saw the monster.

"The opinions of such reliable witnesses is interesting in view of the diversity of opinions as to the reality of the monster."

Gloucestershire Echo - Monday 12 September 1938

Letters To The Editor
THE LOCH NESS MONSTER

Sir, - When I am away from home always have the "Echo" sent on to me, and this afternoon I read in the edition of 8th a notice about the strange creature my sister-in-law, Mrs. Grice-Hutchinson, and myself saw in Loch Ness on Tuesday last.

We were returning from Inverness by car on the lower road, which runs for a long way by the shore of Loch Ness, and when half-way between Dores and Foyers at 2.30 I noticed an object out on the Loch like a large buoy, and as I know the district quite well I wondered what it was, and asked my sister-in-law to pull up.

Greatly to our surprise the object rose out of the water "fore and aft," as one might say, and began to move, at first very slowly, but soon got going at about 15 miles per hour.

I could not see any head or tail, but two large bumps towards the rear. The portion above water I estimated to be about 40 feet long, and at times it rose much more out of the water.

It was going straight down the Loch towards the Inverness end, and at times it turned towards the other shore, when we could only see the bumps. We watched it for some time, and at last it submerged off the ruins of Urquhart Castle.

Two strangers to us who were going towards Inverness had pulled up about 50 yards from us. I asked them if they had a glass, but, unfortunately, neither of us had one. They also had been watching it till it got to Urquhart.

In "The Scotsman" the next day it was reported that some people from Nairn were standing by the Urquhart ruins at 2.35 when they saw the same object we saw, and they saw it submerge. Their description was just as I saw it.

I think it may be of interest to many of your readers to know that there certainly is some very strange living creature in Loch Ness which is not like anything we know. It may be prehistoric. But it is strange and uncommon, consequently some selfish people wish to kill it to satisfy an idle curiosity. I trust the local powers will stop any attempt to destroy it. Some day someone may be close enough with a camera to get a photo of it, that we should know more about it than anyone does at present.

Trusting this lengthy epistle may be of some interest to you.

H. P. DE WINTON, Dell Lodge, Whitebridge, Inverness.
September 9, 1938.

1939

Aberdeen Journal - Friday 26 May 1939

THRILL BY LOCH NESS-SIDE
CLOSE VIEW GOT OF MONSTER
SNAKY NECK WITH POINTED HEAD

The Loch Ness monster reappeared this week, and several onlookers had good views of it.

Its head, neck and one hump were visible.

The creature was watched for more than ten minutes by several persons opposite the Half-Way House Hotel, a mile or two east of Invermoriston.

Among the witnesses were two anglers staying at the Drumnadrochit Hotel, who motored along to visit friends at the Half-Way House, and shortly after arriving they were amazed to see the monster's head and neck appear some thirty yards away.

Mr John Macdonald, of the Royal Hotel, Cupar-Fife, said in an interview that for a moment he thought the creature was an otter, but as about a foot-and-a-half of a snaky neck with a smallish-pointed head were clearly visible all thoughts of an otter vanished. It then dived.

WONDERFUL VIEW

Mr Macdonald added that he was at last convinced that Loch Ness harbours some very strange animal. "Previously," he said, "I frankly admit I was absolutely sceptical.

"The monster came up again," Mr Macdonald added, "and I ran down to the loch side. There it was, only ten yards or so from where I stood, actually looking at me. I was thrilled more than I can say at getting such a wonderful view of the monster, which again showed head, neck and one hump, but again the creature dived, then reappeared in deeper water, and finally out of sight."

The Loch was perfectly calm at the time.

Aberdeen Journal - Friday 23 June 1939

LOCH NESS MONSTER
WATCHED FOR OVER HALF-HOUR
HEAVY HEAD AND NECK

Two Fort-Augustus people watched the Loch Ness monster about ten o'clock on Wednesday night for over half-an-hour.

Mr Thomas Campbell, motor mechanic, and a friend were returning by car from Inverness, and when passing Inverness County Council stonecrushing plant near Loch End they saw the monster's head shoot out of the water only a hundred yards or so from the shore. It was travelling slowly westwards and diving and reappearing. The witnesses had it under full observation for half an hour, during which time it travelled about a mile.

A curious feature of this reappearance was that the witnesses were struck by the thickness of the monster's neck, which many people have described as thin and tapering. They stated that the neck and shoulders appeared to be massive and of heavier build than those of a Clydesdale horse.

Both witnesses declared that judging by the size of the head and neck the monster must be of huge proportions.

Only once before were the monster's head and neck described in this way. This was as long ago as 1934, when the Rev. Murdo Campbell, former Free Church minister of Fort-Augustus, and now of Partick Island Church, Glasgow, said that it reminded him of a bull.

Dundee Evening Telegraph - Tuesday 04 July 1939

"Nessie" Puts On a Show Again
Monster Appears for Several Minutes

Mr William Macdonald, a chauffeur in private service at Fort Augustus, has seen the Loch Ness monster 2½ miles east of Fort Augustus.

Mr Macdonald, accompanied by two other men, was motoring to Inverness, and, when opposite the Horse Shoe, his attention was caught by the appearance of two humps, which were moving slowly along the surface.

He stated that the humps were black and shiny, and each was about seven feet long and three to four feet above water.

He has motored along the loch side for the past nine years, and never believed in the monster's existence till now.

Each hump, he said, was separated by two or three feet of water, and the foremost one was larger than the one behind. The animal, Mr Macdonald declared, is of tremendous proportions.

It travelled towards Glendoe most of the time, and remained in clear view for several minutes before submerging.

Dundee Courier - Wednesday 05 July 1939

New Sea Monster Has Horse's Head Seen by Fife Fishermen

A strange sea monster has taken up its abode in the Firth of Forth.

It was seen yesterday morning in broad daylight by two West Wemyss fishermen.

Like its Loch Ness relative, the monster has a large head and long neck resembling the head and neck of a horse, and big protruding eyes. But no humps were seen.

The monster was spotted basking about 300 yards from the shore just east of West Wemyss by William Christie, South Main Street, and George Salmond, Auld Hoose. They were in the motor boat Reliance, belongng to Christie, and fishing for mackerel.

KEPT STARING.

"We saw the strange thing pop up above the water closer to the shore than we were," said Salmond in an interview.

"We made towards it, and saw that its head and neck were bolt upright out of the water about three feet above the surface. Whenever it saw us it slipped under the surface, but came up again within a minute.

"We circled around it for about an hour, and it kept staring at us except when we got too close, and then it would go under the surface and come up shortly afterwards. When it was down we could follow its wake by the white foam it made while swimming under water."

DARK BROWN.

"Its head was big," declared Christie, and was between the shape of a horse's head and the head of a bear. Its neck was long, and exactly like a horse's. It could turn round at the one spot and watch the movements of the boat without any effort.

"It had big staring eyes, and its skin was very dark brown, also like a horse's, but we couldn't see how long the body or tail was."

Christie has had experience of deep sea fishing in many waters, but has never seen anything even remotely resembling this monster.

Although other fishermen kept a close look-out, it was not seen again.

Dundee Courier - Saturday 05 August 1939

Monster Seen at Close Quarters

An Inverness lady who was out with Mr Donald Munro, a motor car instructor, yesterday had a fine view of the Loch Ness monster as it disported itself in Glenurquhart Bay.

Miss Eva Poole, who resides at Craigside Lodge, Inverness, was driving the car on the Glenalbyn road along Loch Ness side, not far from Urquhart Castle.

Looking out on the loch, Mr Munro observed a huge object in the bay, some 50 or 60 yards away from the shore. It was moving slowly.

He drew Miss Poole's attention to it and both got out of the car and had a clear view.

Indeed, Miss Poole declared – "I could have easily taken a photograph of the monster, it was so near the shore and seemed to be moving very leisurely. I can only describe it as a very huge object. Its back, which had humps, seemed to be like part of an upturned boat. The skin seemed rough and coarse, like that of elephant.

"As Sir Munro and I watched, the monster suddenly turned and moved out towards the middle of the loch. Both of us were excited and Mr Munro, who has been a motor driver for many years, said he had journeyed along Loch Ness side thousand times, but that was the first time he had seen the monster.

"The loch was almost calm as a millpond, and the weather was warm, it being perhaps the sunniest day of the year."

Aberdeen Journal - Monday 07 August 1939

LOCH NESS MONSTER
TWO APPEARANCES REPORTED

A party of motorists journeying along Loch Ness side watched the "monster" for over half an hour at the week-end.

As it cruised slowly on the surface opposite Abriachan pier one of the witnesses, Mrs Gilchrist, whose home is at Eshiels, Peebles, and who is holidaying with her son at Fort-Augustus, stated in an interview that the monster was only thirty yards from the shore when they saw it, and the head, neck, and two humps were clearly visible.

The total length of the body, Mrs Gilchrist said, was about fourteen feet, and quite unlike any other living thing. It reminded her in an odd way of a huge duck. The wash sent out might have come from a small trawler, yet it moved rather slowly, and this more than anything impressed upon her the undoubted power and size of the creature. "We were so thrilled by the sight," Mrs Gilchrist added, "that time was completely forgotten, and we got something of a shock when we found we had actually watched it thirty minutes."

The monster eventually disappeared in the distance near the Foyers shore.

Two Inverness people - Miss Eva Poole, Craigside Lodge, and Mr Donald Munro, a motor car instructor, are also reported to have seen the monster. They observed the creature in Glen Urquhart Bay.

Dundee Evening Telegraph - Thursday 10 August 1939

Monster Obliges Holiday Party

Two London holiday-makers, Mr and Mrs James Jarrows, 150 Wymaring Mansions, Maida Vale, had a close-up view of the Loch Ness monster when they were driving by car towards Inverness on the way to a holiday at Conon.

The couple, who were accompanied by their five-year-old daughter, saw the monster disporting itself in Primrose Bay, near Invermoriston.

On his arrival at Inverness, Mr Jarrows told a reporter that a few minutes before the monster appeared his wife laughingly remarked that she hoped the creature would oblige with an appearance.

"Suddenly," said Mr Jarrows, "about 70 yards from the shore, there was a tremendous commotion. We stopped the car. First a big hump appeared, and after it had risen about a foot out of the water, two more portions of the monster, presumably the head and tail, came into view.

"It was about 60 yards away when it first appeared, and after a few minutes it began to move towards the centre of the loch. Its movement through the water was so smooth that I am sure it must swim by means of fins.

"My only regret," concluded Mr Jarrows, "is that we did not have a camera with a telescopic lens with us, because I could then easily have taken a photograph that would have enabled the creature to be recognised."

Aberdeen Journal - Monday 14 August 1939

HAS "NESSIE" MIGRATED?

The inevitable "Loch Ness Monster" has reared its head - this time in the waters off Queen Charlotte Islands, British Columbia.

Local fishermen have reported on several occasions that they have seen an enormous marine monster, reputedly a large eel with antenna on each side of a head shaped rather like that of the sea lion.

The serpent is said to have been seen rearing its head and body about ten feet above water.

When breathing on the surface it is said to make a noise like a high-powered aeroplane. It is alleged to be dark brown in colour and to be addicted to the playful habit of tossing seals into the air before eating them.

Hartlepool Mail - Wednesday 16 August 1939

LOCH NESS MONSTER
Holidaymaker Says it had Three Humps

Four people watched the Loch Ness monster for three-quarters of an hour at Fort Augustus yesterday afternoon.

They are Mr. and Mrs. James Duguid. of 26 Carfrae Park, Edinburgh, their 16-year-old son, and Mrs. Herbert Fraser, with whom they are spending their holiday at Fort Augustus.

Mr. Duguid said that when they were standing near the mouth of the River Oich the monster appeared.

One hump, 10ft long and 4ft high, was in view, but presently the hump revealed itself into three distinct humps.

Then fully 10ft. ahead of the foremost hump, the monster's head and neck appeared, the head being sharp-pointed and shaped like that of a collie dog.

All this time the animal was swimming slowly against a stiff wind, and, in doing so, showed several flippers working with an up-and-down motion, churning the water into foam.

The monster set off in the direction of Inverness and was finally lost to view.

Mr Duguid took a snapshot of the animal but fears it will not be much good as the camera is a very small one and the animal was about 200 yards away.

He said the whole thing was an extraordinary spectacle.

Aberdeen Journal - Wednesday 30 August 1939

LOCH NESS MONSTER AGAIN WATCHED BY MEN IN BOAT

Glasgow men on holiday at St Benedict's Abbey, Fort-Augustus, and a monk of the abbey had an excellent view of the Loch Ness monster near Fort-Augustus.

In an interview, Mr W. Bradley, of Westmuir Street, Parkhead, Glasgow, said that the monster suddenly appeared near Glendoe Boathouse, when Mr Bradley and his two companions were out for a row in a small boat.

The monster was then 250 yards away, two large humps being clearly visible. It remained in view for four minutes, then dived, sending out a considerable wash.

Shortly afterwards it reappeared, and Mr Bradley rowed the boat towards it, hoping to make a sketch of the head and neck and humps, as no camera was available. The monster remained on the surface long enough for this to be done, then, becoming aware of the boat's approach. it made off in a different direction.

The three witnesses were positive of three things:- The monster really exists in Loch Ness, its head is like that of a horse in shape and size, and its total length is between twenty-five and thirty feet.

1940s

Aberdeen Journal - Monday 08 April 1940

Loch Ness Monster Appears Again

After being in hiding since last summer, the Loch Ness monster reappeared yesterday to give the occupants of five motor cars a first-rate view of it.

Appearing shortly after midday off Primrose Bay, Invermoriston, the monster stayed on the surface for fully fifteen minutes before it went off in the direction of Fort-Augustus, and then disappeared.

The party which first saw the monster yesterday included Mr James Matthews, solicitor's clerk, of 5 Hutton Place, Edinburgh, who was driving towards Inverness with his wife, his sixteen-year-old son, and his brother, Mr Herbert Matthews.

"We were within a mile or two of Invermoriston village," Mr Matthews told a "Press and Journal" representative, "when I noticed a black-looking object on the surface of the water about 100 yards from the shore.

TREMENDOUS COMMOTION

"I pointed it out to the other occupants of the car, and my wife cried excitedly 'It's the monster.' We stopped at once, and immediately we got out we saw a tremendous commotion close to the object.

"Even this did not convince me that it was the monster, but a few seconds later we saw a thin neck rising several feet out of the water.

"That convinced us all, and as we looked at it it seemed that the beast was eating something because the neck was repeatedly bent down into the water and raised again.

"Shortly afterwards we stopped four other cars which came on the scene, and all the occupants came out to watch the monster."

ABOUT 30 FEET LONG

Mr Matthews added that he estimated the length of the beast at about thirty feet and its width between two to three feet.

"I looked for the humps about which so many people have spoken," he continued, "but I could not see them.

"At times the monster seemed to lower part of its back into the loch, and I think this may have given others the impression of humps.

"It moved off quickly in the direction Fort-Augustus, causing considerable commotion in the water, and then it seemed gradually to sink out of sight."

"A great thrill," was how Mrs Matthews described the monster's appearance.

"We are doing a week's tour of the Highlands, and you can imagine how glad we are to be able to go home and tell our friends that we have seen the famous monster.

"This is not our first visit to Loch Ness, but although I have looked for it on every previous occasion this is the first time that I have had any luck."

Aberdeen Journal - Thursday 30 May 1940

The Loch Ness monster was seen by a party of three yesterday for about ten minutes. It appeared to be feeding. The spectators saw two large humps, and a small head moving up and down as if the animal were feeding.

Aberdeen Journal - Thursday 18 July 1940

Three holidaymakers from Oban got a ten-minutes' view of the Loch Ness monster near Invermoriston yesterday forenoon. It was about forty yards from the shore and seemed to be about thirty feet long with a black shiny skin and two humps, at least three feet in height, on its back.

Yorkshire Evening Post - Friday 02 August 1940

WHAT OF LOCH NESS?

It is a long time since we heard tell of the monster of Loch Ness (writes a gossip in the "Scotsman") The time has now come when one of those indefatigable M.P.s who ask questions in the House about the whereabouts of individuals might demand information on the monster. It is unthinkable that the Government could have granted an exent permit to this creature whose behaviour during times of peace entitled it to little consideration.

There may, of course, be good and solid reasons why we should be kept in ignorance of the monster's activities. It is quite possible that, camouflaged and stripped for action, it has been engaged on useful war work. It may have been doing convoy work in Northern waters, or may have been engaged on reconnaissance patrols.

Dundee Courier - Monday 18 August 1941

LOCH NESS MONSTER TURNS UP AGAIN
Thrilling Display of High Spirits

After months of inactivity, the Loch Ness monster was seen near Fort-Augustus at the week-end by Mr J. Macfarlane-Barrow, Fort-Augustus, and three of his children.

A yachting enthusiast, Mr Macfarlane-Barrow was sailing with the children on the loch in his yacht dinghy when they saw the monster appear close by Glendoe Pier.

A long snaky neck and from 15 to 18 feet of the body, shaped rather like an upturned boat, was clearly visible for ten minutes.

The witnesses said the monster gave a thrilling display as it raced up and down, then across the loch, diving and reappearing with the agility of a seabird. It threw up a column of water, and in Miss Macfarlane-Barrow's own words, seemed to be in high spirits.

Altogether the monster covered the best part of seven miles during its display, and it finally dived out of sight about half a mile from Fort-Augustus.

Dundee Evening Telegraph - Thursday 21 August 1941

LOCH NESS MONSTER TWICE SEEN SCHOOLMASTER AND WIFE WITNESSES

Whether the weather has had anything do with it or not, the Loch Ness monster appears to have entered upon another period of activity, having twice risen from the depths since it was sighted few days ago by Mr J. MacFarlane-Barrow, Erins, Port Augustus, and his three children.

The latest witnesses include Mr I. Cook, retired headmaster of a large Glasgow primary school, who, on account of the present scarcity of teachers, has resumed duty. He is now in charge of between 30 and 40 Glasgow school children who were three weeks ago evacuated, as part of their school, to Glendoe Lodge, Fort Augustus.

Mr Cook, who was accompanied by his wife, saw the monster from fine vantage-point on the drive which connects the lodge with the main road to Fort Augustus, twice within the past few days, obtaining an excellent view of it on both occasions.

In an interview, he admitted that he had been a confirmed sceptic on this subject until recently, but Mrs Cook always believed there must be something very odd in the loch. He and his wife were walking soon after nine o'clock in the evening down the drive, and having walked only a quarter of a mile they saw the monster come to the surface.

"This animal, whatever it may be, had the appearance of an upturned boat. It moved diagonally away from us - roughly towards the River Oich - but the rate of speed was not easily determined. I should say it moved faster than a rowing boat, leaving a distinct wake. It was about 18 feet long. We watched for about seven minutes; then it dived, throwing up big splash and a flurry of foam."

400 Yards Away.

The next time Mr and Mrs Cook saw the monster they were joined by Robert Howden, a 12-year-old Fort Augustus schoolboy. This time the three witnesses saw the animal less than 400 yards distant, and again from the drive, which rises steeply above the loch level, and affords a really good view of a large expanse of water.

Mr Cook, describing the second appearance, said the creature had the form of "a dark, slow-moving substance." "Then, with incredible speed, it suddenly dashed forward some hundred yards, raising a thick, dark neck and head, high out of the water. Just as suddenly, it disappeared.

"In its dash it produced a wide wake and a great commotion in the waters. The neck was about four feet long, and as far as I could judge its thickness would be about eight inches, but it seemed to be about the same diameter all the way up, and I could not say that it showed any pronounced taper.

On returning to the lodge, Mr Cook drew up a detailed record of what he had seen, with rough sketches of the monster's body and neck.

Portsmouth Evening News - Friday 22 August 1941

Canadian Loch Ness Monster

VERNON. B.C.: Okanagan Lake's Ogopogo - a Canadian version of the Loch Ness monster - has made one of its rare appearances, according to two young girls.

While in a rowing boat they say they saw a snake-like head and a 30-foot looped tail coming towards them through a swirl water.

The existence of "Ogopogo" is chronicled in an Indian legend dating back from long before the white man's arrival.

Aberdeen Journal - Monday 26 January 1942

Orkney 'Monster' Mystery

A twenty-four-foot carcase of a "monster" has been washed ashore at Deepdale, in the parish of Holm, in the Orkney Islands.

The carcase, badly decomposed, has not been identified, but it resembles that of the extinct plesiosaurus, a marine animal allied to the lizard and crocodile, and remarkable for the length of neck.

It will shortly be examined by experts.

The new "find" may revive theories about the Loch Ness monster, which some people thought was a surviving plesiosaurus.

Aberdeen Journal - Friday 06 February 1942

LAND, SEA AND LOCH MONSTERS
(To the Editor)

Sir,- The existence or otherwise of land, loch, or sea "monsters" is always a fascinating subject, and a continuous source of argument between those who have seen and those who have not. The washing up on a beach of the Orkney Islands of the carcase of another "monster" revives the controversy, and the professors of our Natural History Departments are faced with another problem to solve.

The Keeper of Zoology at the Natural History Museum, London, states that the "monster" is a basking shark, but the photograph in your issue does not warrant that view. Mr Walter G. Grant, an Orkney antiquary, thinks it might be a prehistoric plesiosaurus, and a brother of the Loch Ness monster. Both Mr Robert Elmhirst, chief of Scottish Marine Biological Station, Isle of Cumbrae, and Professor Ritchie, Chair of Natural History, Edinburgh University, deny the possibility of the "monster" being a plesiosaurus, but with all respect to these gentlemen their opinions are based only upon an assumption that such monsters became extinct some forty million years ago. Land monsters of the Jurassic Age may have become extinct then, but it does not follow that plesiosauri, which were vegetarian amphibians, did so.

TWO IN LOCH NESS

In 1934 my wife and I and two children spent a week-end at Loch Ness in the hope of catching a glimpse of the alleged elusive "monster." The first night there, at about 6.30 p.m., we were amazed to see not one "monster" but TWO break the surface of the loch at a point immediately opposite what is locally called "Johnnie's Point."

Only their necks were visible, estimated at about eight feet long, and their heads appeared to resemble and to be the size of that of a cow. The TWO "monsters" remained visible for at least twenty minutes, approached the far side of the loch one at a time, and appeared to eat, chased each other about, and then disappeared at different times beneath the surface about half-a-mile from where they first appeared.

In 1934 a well-known daily newspaper was very interested in the existence of the "monster" and I reported the facts most fully at the time, but beyond a brief acknowledgment of my letter, the news editor thought my report so far fetched that he declined to publish it. Nevertheless the facts were truthfully reported.

LIKE ANCIENT CREATURES

Since being a witness of two live unclassified "monsters" of Loch Ness, I have diligently studied the history of all monsters known to have inhabited the earth, and the more I have done so, the more I personally am convinced that the "monsters" in Loch Ness, if not actually survivors from a prehistoric age, at least resemble to a great degree of accuracy the accepted representation of what a plesiosaurus looked like when alive.

It is to be hoped that the "monsters," whatever they are, will multiply and survive the war, so that when peace descends to earth all parties interested may make an exhaustive effort to solve once and for all the nature and species of these denizens of Loch Ness. - Robert Neish, Craigisla, Peterhead.

Gloucester Citizen - Monday 09 August 1943

The Loch Ness monster, front page figure in peace-time, has reared its head again, according to local inhabitants.

Aberdeen Journal - Saturday 26 February 1944

Missing Monster

Commander Gould put across a pretty piece of publicity for Inverness-shire when, as a member of the Brains Trust he expressed the fixed belief that "the Loch Ness monster does, or DID, exist." His conviction is founded on personal interrogation of about sixty eye-witnesses and on photographs showing undulant humps threshing through spray.

Mr Emanuel Shinwell, M.P., also on the Brains Trust, was sceptical concerning the monster, but pertinently remarked, "Anyhow it brings a lot of profit to people in the neighbourhood" – "it," in his case, evidently implying "legend."

What is of importance is whether the creature, for long months now unobserved, still inhabits the loch or has returned to the sea. Has a first-class, unduplicated attraction to tourists ceased to be a money-yielding asset to a county which aspires to post-war record popularity with holidaymakers?

We trust that the answer is "No" both to this question and to the query, "Was It Nessie?" which headed a recent news item stating that a myopic or playful sea-monster had been in violent collision with a submarine. Only minor damage was done to the craft, but an ominous sentence read, "No carcase was seen, but hull plates were covered with black slime which emitted a strong fish-like smell."

Aberdeen Weekly Journal - Thursday 13 April 1944

Loch Ness Monster

Apprehension that the famous Loch Ness monster had forsaken its established dwelling-place or, as was suggested, that it had met a tragic end, has been dispelled by the announcement that a Fort Augustus woman has had the creature under observation recently.

After an unusually long period of non-appearance it has, with the advent of Spring, come to the surface of the loch and disported itself as of yore by making a characteristic undulating dash through the water, "sending out a wash like that from a steamer."

With restrictions on the use of cameras the monster is less likely to be stalked meantime by amateur photographers than in the days when reports of frequent frolics drew many watchers to the loch in the hope of catching a glimpse of the leviathan and snapping evidence of its existence to convince the incredulous.

Loch Ness may be able to provide a post-war attraction to visitors for many years to come. The pity is that the prospect of further performances this season is unlikely to benefit the district financially to anything like the extent that would have obtained in normal times.

Aberdeen Journal - Tuesday 04 July 1944

U.S. Rival to "Nessie"

New York. Monday. A rival of the Loch Ness monster has made another reappearance at Payette Lake, Idaho, and this time has been reported by two independent observers.

The "monster," described as being thirty-five feet long, yellow with humps on the back, has been "reappearing" for ten years. Mrs George Van Steeg, a guest at a nearby hotel, said the monster broke surface, so she examined it closely with binoculars and was able to confirm previous descriptions.

Walter Bowling, hotel proprietor, who formerly scoffed at the serpent's existence, was walking along the lake shore and saw it simultaneously. He said it seemed as big as a whale.

Aberdeen Journal - Saturday 19 August 1944

Irish Rival to Loch Ness?

A strange monster, estimated to be 15 feet long and diving with a rumbling noise, is disturbing the peace of Lake Dromate, near New Bliss, Co. Monaghan.

It has already attracted a large number of people to the lake and may rival the fame of the Loch Ness monster.

It is said to have been seen several times.

It was first noticed by some men fishing from the lake shore. It appeared as a black patch a few inches above the water.

Local farmers armed with shot guns entered a boat to search for it, and to their astonishment it broke surface about twenty yards from the boat.

Only a portion of it, about two feet square, was visible at first, but from the way the water was disturbed it is estimated to measure about fifteen feet.

One man fired both barrels of his shot gun at the creature, which rose partly out of the water and then dived underneath with a rumbling noise.

Two hours later it reappeared in a different part of the lake and was again fired at by a farmer. Although six shots altogether have been fired, it continues to appear.

Gloucester Citizen - Thursday 05 October 1944

"LOCH NESS MONSTER" IN BURMA

Burma said to have its own "Loch Ness monster."

A number of Major-General Lentaigne's men of the 3rd Indian Division claim to have seen it. The haunt of this alleged giant-like creature is Indawgyi Lake, the 15-mile long stretch of water 20 miles to the west of Mogaung, and recently in the news as the base for the Sunderland flying boat operation which played such a successful part in this year's North Burma campaign.

Describing how he first spotted the monster, Capt. John P. Lee-Warner, Recce Corps, whose home is at Seagrave near Loughborough, Leicestershire, said he was crossing the lake in a motorboat with three other men when he saw "two large bumps" sticking out of the water 50 yards away.

Depth Charges

"Blimey, it's the Loch Ness monster!" said one of his companions as they turned the boat towards the bumps, which created a wash as they moved through the water at full speed. The little engine was not fast enough, however, and the "monster" disappeared. Using hand grenades as depth charges, the party swept the area in an "antisubmarine" attack but only a few dead fish came to the surface.

The story quickly got around and soon others claimed to have seen the serpent-like bumps. Capt. Lee-Warner told his story to the headman of Chaugwa, whose opinion was that it was a large crocodile.

Another very unofficial theory is that the monster is none other than the legendary Burmese griffon, with eagle's head and wings and lion's body which the 3rd Indian Division Chindits have adopted as their badge.

Aberdeen Journal - Monday 21 May 1945

Nessie Again

After having been out of sight for fully thirteen months, the Loch Ness monster has been seen disporting herself again with-undiminished abandon. Several persons agree that she surfaced like a submarine, threshed along with an undulating motion leaving a wake resembling that of torpedo travelling at high speed, and then submerged "quickly and neatly."

Everyone who gives credence to Nessie's existence will agree that her periodical appearances are well-timed to whet public interest just when the holiday season is approaching.

While U-boats may be made public peep-shows for a time, the Monster, if she "does her stuff" with reasonable frequency, need have no fear that she will be other than a star attraction, particularly as she levies no fee!

Aberdeen Journal - Thursday 12 July 1945

SWEDISH RIVAL TO LOCH NESS MONSTER

A giant sea serpent closely resembling the Loch Ness monster was seen near the shore in Lake Storsjoe, Central Sweden, on Sunday, according to the Stockholm "Tidningen."

Three reputedly reliable witnesses were sitting near the shore of the lake when its calm shining surface began to boil about fifty yards from the shore. The surface was then broken by a giant snake-like monster with three prickly dark humps.

According to the paper the creature swam at a good speed parallel with the shore, causing waves to break. The three people ran to the shore of the lake, but the "serpent" disappeared. A little while later it broke the surface again, but once more disappeared.

Another "Storsjoe Monster" is reported to have been seen in the same spot about ten years ago. The lake well stocked with fish, but is only about 90 feet deep.

Dundee Evening Telegraph - Tuesday 09 July 1946

Monster Season Opens

The Loch Ness monster's first appearance this year is reported by four Elgin men who were motoring by the loch. Display lasted five minutes.

Aberdeen Journal - Monday 29 July 1946

LOCH NESS MONSTER MAKES REAPPEARANCE
Cruising at 20 Miles an Hour, Says Inverness Man

Early yesterday morning a party of four motoring along Loch Ness saw what they believe to be the Loch Ness Monster.

Two of the party were Inverness men, Mr D. A. Campbell, 11 Kingsmills Road, and Mr M. McKenzie, 46 Telford Road, who were both recently demobilised from the Army.

Along with two Glasgow holiday-makers, Miss Ann Scott and Miss Helen McClure, they were driving along the lochside admiring the scenery.

"Suddenly," said Mr Campbell to a representative of "The Press and Journal," "I saw a huge black head in the centre of the loch.

"I drew the attention of the rest of the party to it and stopped the car. We rushed to the bank, and for two minutes watched the monster cruising up the loch at about twenty miles an hour.

"All that was visible was the large, horse-like head and neck, which gradually submerged.

"I was often kidded about the monster when I was serving in the desert, but was always sceptical about its existence," added Mr Campbell.

Mr McKenzie said there was no doubt that what they saw was some sort of creature of large proportions.

The monster was last reported to have been seen on Sunday, July 7.

On that occasion, four Bishopmill (Elgin) men motoring along the banks of the loch, watched the creature for five minutes. One of them described what he saw as similar to the dragon head of a Viking ship.

Aberdeen Journal - Tuesday 08 April 1947

LOCH NESS MONSTER SHOWS ITS PACE
'Like Speed-boat,' Says Inverness County Clerk

After an absence of several months the Loch Ness monster has made a reappearance - this time near Drumnadrochit.

It has been seen by two parties of motorists who were travelling along the side of the loch.

One of the motorists, Mr J. W. MacKillop, county clerk of Inverness-shire, told a reporter of "The Press and Journal": "I saw a long white streak in water, like foam from a speedboat, and I drew the attention of my friends to it and stopped the car.

"The object made its way across to the Foyers side of the loch at tremendous speed."

"We watched it for a considerable time since it was quite near to us, and had it not been for the fact that there was no sound of an engine I would have taken it for a speed boat."

Disappeared

Mr MacKillop was accompanied by his son, Normand, and an English friend, both of whom are on leave from the Army.

The other party of motorists who saw the monster were Mr Lystan Lamb, a stage artist, and his wife and her sister, who were members of a variety company appearing at the Empire Theatre, Inverness, last week, and Mr J. Fraser, joiner, Denny Street, Inverness.

In their description they also spoke of the tremendous wash caused by the object as it sped from one side of the loch to the other.

Dundee Courier - Tuesday 08 April 1947

Monster Season Opens

A party from Inverness, motoring alongside Loch Ness at the week-end, saw a commotion in the water.

A long wake was streaming from a big black object. The motorists came to the conclusion that the monster was making one of its rare appearances.

The loch was calm and the sun was shining brightly.

The car was driven by Mr J. W. McKillop, county clerk of Inverness-shire, and he was accompanied by his son Norman, home on leave from the army, and Mr Kenneth Cottier, an Englishman, also on leave.

They said that near Drumnadrochit they saw a big dark object with humps. They watched fully five minutes as it moved at terrific speed up the loch. Then it disappeared.

"I had no doubt," said Mr McKillop, "that there was something abnormal in the water and that it was what people describe as the monster."

"It was my first visit to Loch Ness," said Mr Cottier. "I had a clear view of the loch, and observed at the head of the long white wake two humps, the first being the larger.

"I followed its progress on the surface for at least five minutes before it disappeared."

Dundee Courier - Tuesday 08 April 1947

LEGEND OF THE LOCH

Cynics will smile knowingly over the news that the Loch Ness monster has just staged its first ceremonial post-war appearance.

A nice attraction for the Easter visitors, they will remark, and timely publicity for the hoped-for influx of summer holidaymakers - especially dollar-bearing tourists.

But the latest eye-witness report on the mysterious denizen of the loch is not to be lightly dismissed. The county clerk of Inverness-shire puts his evidence with legal caution. He has no doubt there was something abnormal in the water and that it was "what people describe as the monster."

His son, home on army leave, and an English companion were explicit about the dark object with the familiar humps, and watched its progress for fully five minutes.

Whatever "Nessie" may be, it is something more than a hallucination. Yet - is it perhaps better unidentified in the light of common day?

We badly need those tourists' dollars.

Dundee Courier - Friday 02 May 1947

COUNCIL HEARS ABOUT LOCH NESS MONSTER

Inverness County Council suspended Standing Orders yesterday to hear the County Clerk (Mr J. W. McKillop) describe how he saw the Loch Ness monster.

Mr McKillop confessed he had had a certain amount of doubt about the monster's existence, but all his doubts were dispelled when he had the good fortune while motoring along Loch Ness to see the monster.

"I firmly convinced," said Mr McKillop, "there is something quite abnormal in the depth of the loch.

"It is capable of extraordinary speed, and creates a disturbance in the water that would suggest it must be of immense proportions."

MINISTER SAW IT

The County Clerk added that the chairman of the Education Committee, Rev. William Graham, Ardersier, had seen the monster on a previous occasion.

Rev. Mr Graham - Nobody would believe me. (Laughter.) They would not even believe when I said I saw it from a tearoom and not from a hotel. (Laughter.)

Sir D. W. Cameron of Lochiel, county convener, said he had been sceptical about the monster, but was convinced of its existence now. There could no more trustworthy witness than the County Clerk.

Mr F. W. Walker of Leys Castle suggested the monster should be made an honorary member of Inverness County Council, but Lochiel replied there was no provision for that in the Local Government Act.

14 YEARS OLD NOW

It was in 1933 that the story first came to an incredulous world of a monster making its home in the depths of Loch Ness and occasionally coming to the surface.

In one four-week period in 1934 21 people claimed to have spotted it.

Scientists have said it might be a seal or a giant eel, but Bertram Mills hoped for more than that. In 1934 he offered £20,000 for it, and that offer led to it being quoted at Lloyd's.

Aberdeen Journal - Friday 09 May 1947

Spotters to Keep Vigil for "Nessie"

The spotting post established at a cottage at Loch Ness, four miles from Dores, for the purpose of keeping a vigil for the monster, is to be well manned.

Volunteers are daily approaching Mr A. B. Peters, Inverness Burgh Museum curator and librarian, who is sponsoring the plan, with offers to do spells of duty.

"It has certainly attracted widespread interest," he told "The Press and Journal" yesterday. "In fact, the number of people volunteering - young and old - to assist is proving embarrassing.

"Still, it is certain that the long-range telescope which I have set up in a commanding position above the loch will be manned from dawn to dusk all summer."

Mr Peters believes, however, that to achieve the best results a chain of observation posts should be established all along the loch.

Aberdeen Journal - Wednesday 14 May 1947

"N FOR NESSIE" TO COMB LOCH FOR MONSTER

The next move by Mr A. B. Peters, Inverness librarian and curator of Inverness Burgh Museum, in his bid to establish the identity of the Loch Ness monster, will be a plane flight along Loch Ness in the hope of locating the creature.

Along with Mr I. Stewart, an actor and poet, Mr Peters has already established an observation post on the shores of Loch Ness, where a powerful telescope is manned from dawn to dusk.

"I will choose a clear day when observation is good," Mr Peters told a reporter of "The Press and Journal" yesterday, "and hope that I may be able to spot the monster.

"I am also taking a seventeen-year-old French girl, who is at present attending Inverness Academy, on the flight with me."

At the observation post, Mr Stewart told our reporter yesterday that so far there is nothing to report. Mr Peters and he had already received many letters from people in Scotland and England offering advice and asking questions.

Dundee Courier - Thursday 15 May 1947

Nessie Disports For The Ladies

From the window of their motor caravan yesterday two girls had a three-minute view of the Loch Ness monster disporting itself about 300 yards from the shore near Drumnadrochit.

The girls were Misses Julie and Vera Gray, who were being driven by their father, Mr Thomas Gray, amusement caterer, The Showground, Drumnadrochit.

Miss Julie described the monster being of tremendous size. Its tail, which seemed to thrash the water, was, in her estimation, about 20 feet long.

She said her sister and she had been very sceptical about the monster story and they could hardly believe their eyes when it appeared. Sometimes it lifted its tail right out of the water. Unfortunately it was too far out to see many details.

She shouted to her father to stop the car but he could not hear her. He was very disappointed when told about it.

Aberdeen Journal - Thursday 15 May 1947

"Nessie" Up for 3-minute Breather

The Loch Ness monster re-appeared for three minutes near Drumnadrochit yesterday afternoon. It was watched through the window of a motor caravan by two girls travelling towards Glen Urquhart.

The girls, Julie and Vera Gray, were travelling in the caravan driven by their father, Mr T. Gray, amusement caterer, The Showground, Drumnadrochit.

When "Nessie" made her unexpected appearance they tried to get their father to stop the caravan, but were unable to attract his attention in the driving seat.

Here is what Julie told a reporter of "The Press and Journal" last night:-

"We watched 'Nessie' for fully three minutes. She is a tremendous size, and her tail, with which she seemed to lash the water, must be about 20 feet long.

"The monster first appeared about 300 yards out, near l)rumnadrochit, and for three minutes raced along the surface of the loch.

Exceptionally Speedy

"Sometimes she lifted her tail right out of the water. Her description? - Colossal; black, and exceptionally speedy. It was like nothing I had ever seen before, but 'Nessie' was too far out to see many details."

Disappointed when told of the monster's appearance, almost directly opposite his cottage on the side of the loch, was Mr I. Stewart, actor and painter, who continues to maintain a lonely vigil at the observation post set up in the hope of seeing and identifying the creature.

He said last night that he had been scanning the loch all day with his powerful telescope, but visibility was very limited because of a heavy mist.

Aberdeen Journal - Tuesday 20 May 1947

BROADCAST TO U.S. ON MONSTER?
Invitation to M.P. for Inverness-shire

Sir Murdoch Macdonald, M.P. for Inverness-shire, has not yet made a decision whether to accept the invitation of an American radio company to broadcast a talk to America on the Loch Ness monster.

He told a reporter of "The Press and Journal" yesterday that he had to see an official of the American company in London after the Whitsun recess, when he will discuss the proposed broadcast.

"I will give him all the facts," Sir Murdoch said, "and if the material is suitable I will make a recording of what I have to say."

Despite the views of the sceptics, Sir Murdoch is convinced that there is a strange creature in the loch. "My son and I saw it one beautiful, clear summer day prior to the war, when the loch was like a mill pond," he added.

Meanwhile many Invernessians spent yesterday, the annual May holiday, on Loch Ness-side in the hope of seeing "Nessie," but there were no reports that the monster had come to the surface.

Aberdeen Journal - Thursday 22 May 1947

"Nessie" Shy of Spotter Plane

"Nessie" did not oblige when Mr A. B. Peters, curator of Inverness Museum, made his planned flight over Loch Ness in the hope of seeing the monster.

For an hour the plane cruised over the loch at a height of just over 1000ft., and although conditions were perfect there was not a sign of the elusive inhabitant.

Mr Peters told a reporter of "The Press and Journal" yesterday that he had chosen the time for his flight when conditions were similar to those under which the monster had most frequently been seen.

"Conditions were perfect," he said. "There was not a ripple on the surface and had there been any [???]

object floating about we would have picked it up right away. We patrolled the loch for about an hour at a height of just over a thousand feet, but the monster did not oblige."

Nevertheless, Mr Peters is not discouraged by the failure of his efforts to see the monster since the establishment of his observation post on Loch Ness-side over a month ago.

"It may take hundreds of hours of patient observation before we are successful," he said, "but I think in the end that we shall achieve our object – the identification of the creature."

Accompanying Mr Peters in his monster-spotting flight was Mlle. Paulette Sicard, seventeen-year-old French schoolgirl.

"I am convinced there is something in the loch," she said, "and I intend cycling up Loch Ness-side as much as I can in the hope of seeing the monster."

Monster, or -- ?

What is the truth about the Loch Ness Monster? Is the whole thing just ballyhoo, or is there really something there?

Jack Adrian, the wide-awake "Evening Express" columnist, has come to Inverness to inquire for himself, and in t-night's paper he will tell frankly what he saw and what he thinks about it.

Aberdeen Journal - Monday 02 June 1947

"Nessie" Cruises Loch for Nearly an Hour Like a Giant Python, Says Inverness Man

The Loch Ness monster went for a fifty-five minute surface cruise on Saturday afternoon.

It was watched by a party of Inverness motorists who followed "Nessie's" progress for about a mile until it finally submerged.

It was the second time one of the party – Mr A. Mackenzie, Montague Row, Inverness – had seen the monster and he told a reporter of "The Press and Journal" that three humps and a head were distinctly visible.

"After the monster broke the surface," he said, "we chased it by car for a distance of about a mile until it eventually submerged.

"I estimated its length at about thirty-five feet. It was dark and shiny and was for all the world like a giant python."

"Nessie's" Saturday afternoon cruise was also watched by Mrs R. Gordon from the door of her house at Brackla, on the loch-side.

She told our representative that the monster was too far out to be seen clearly and visibility was bad.

"This is the second time I have seen the monster," she said, "and it has also been seen by my mother and grandfather."

Aberdeen Journal - Tuesday 03 June 1947

Monster-Hunters Told By Curator - "Nessie" Cannot be Captured

A two-man expedition which has been formed to capture the elusive camera-shy Loch Ness monster may give rise to a legal quibble.

Following the announcement yesterday that the two men are preparing plans for the "big game" hunt, Mr A. B. Peters, curator of Inverness Burgh Library and Museum, issued advice to the would-be monster-catchers to ascertain the legal position before launching "Operation Nessie."

According to Mr Peters, the loch's denizen of the deep has the law on her side.

As far back as 1933, he told a reporter of "The Press and Journal," it became a protected creature.

Police Order

"At that time," he said, "the police were informed that under no circumstances was anyone to be allowed to interfere with the strange creature resident in Loch Ness.

"It seems that it can be watched and photographed, should anyone be so fortunate, but captured - no.

"I would therefore strongly advise any prospective monster-hunters to make sure of the legal position before taking any definite action."

Aberdeen Journal - Friday 06 June 1947

Loch Ness Monster

Sir,- Your report on the Loch Ness Monster amused me.

The tourist's (from India) description of "Nessie" makes her more absurd still.

"The Monster looked shiny!" How could any object that is wet look otherwise?

"It resembled a giant python about thirty-five feet long." Even if the tourist could judge its length from the distance he was from it, how could he see the markings that made it look like a python, and where ever did he see a python with three humps on its back?

Pythons are common at thirty feet long. I have heard of them being over forty feet, and actually saw one killed at Buradighi T.E., Dooars (Bengal), thirty-two feet long; so why a giant python?

Na, na, Nessie's description is getting "worser and worser."

It will be interesting to see what the laddie catches with his patent line and hooks - but what's wrong with a net? - D. S. Allan, Aberdeen.

Aberdeen Journal - Thursday 19 June 1947

'NESSIE' WAVES HER TAIL AT BOY ANGLERS

Two young anglers fishing in Loch Ness last night had a better fishing tale than usual to tell their friends. They saw the Loch Ness monster.

The boys, Peter Bennett, aged fifteen, West Lodge, and seventeen-year-old Alexander Marshall, Balnacraig, Inverness, were fishing from Abriachan Pier on the Drumnadrochit side of the loch when "Nessie" appeared and sped along the surface for five minutes.

"We had an excellent view," said the boys. "We counted six or seven humps and estimated that it must have been about seventy feet long. Unfortunately it seemed to keep its head well under the water, but sometimes it lashed the water with its tail."

Several motorists travelling along the side of the loch stopped to watch the monster disporting itself.

Aberdeen Journal - Tuesday 29 July 1947

"Six Humps" Says Witness
"NESSIE" SHOWS HER SPEED

A tremendous splash which disturbed a party of picnickers on the opposite side of Loch Ness almost a mile away heralded the appearance of the Loch Ness Monster for the first time for over a month.

The picnickers were Mr George Forbes, an Inverness banker, of Old Edinburgh Road, his wife and two friends, Miss A. Munford, Glasgow, and Miss E. [???], Guernsey.

"We were sitting by the side of the loch about six miles from Foyers, when we heard a splash," declared Mrs Forbes. "On looking over the loch, we saw several large black humps about a mile away near the other side.

"Tremendous Speed"

"They were moving at a tremendous speed towards the Fort Augustus end of the loch, and set up such a wash that the waves were splashing in the air when they ran ashore at our side, although previously the loch had been as calm as a pond.

"After travelling about half a mile the monster turned and came across towards our side of the loch.

"We could then see six black shiny humps or coils as the creature writhed through the water like a huge serpent. It seemed to be over thirty feet long, but we could see no head."

Mrs Forbes added that when the monster turned towards them she jumped up and got ready to run, but the monster then disappeared.

Aberdeen Journal - Monday 18 August 1947

Will 'Nessie' Become Circus Draw?

Mr Lambert, representing the Bertram Mills world-famous circus and menagerie which opens for a week at Inverness to-day, went on a mission of inquiry during the week-end to see if any light could be thrown on some knotty questions concerning the Loch Ness monster.

The reason for this is that the directors of Bertram Mills are seriously considering making a fresh offer for the capture of the monster. A final decision is expected within a day or two.

"Firstly, has anyone the right to remove the monster?" asks Mr Lambert, "and secondly, would the offer now under consideration, if and when made operative, constitute an incitement to an illegal act?

"It is important that in a matter of this kind nothing should be done that would constitute a breach of any regulations," he said.

In 1938, Bertram Mills offered £20,000 for the delivery of the monster alive, by January, 1939.

Ruling Asked

Mr Lambert had a talk with Mr R. Gilbert, clerk to the Ness District Fishery Board, which has certain rights in Loch Ness, but as an official of the Board Mr Gilbert said he was not prepared to make any statement regarding the issues raised.

After this meeting Mr Lambert said: "It would now be well if someone in high authority would give a ruling regarding these points."

At Inverness yesterday it was ascertained that the instruction issued by the Crown authorities still held good, namely, that the police should see to it that no harm should come to the monster.

Aberdeen Journal - Tuesday 19 August 1947

£20,000 Offer for "Nessie"

Mr Cyril Mills, of Bertram J. Mills' Circus and Menagerie, now at Inverness, announced yesterday that the firm has again decided to offer £20,000 for the capture and delivery alive of the Loch Ness monster by January, 1948.

Nevertheless, when Provost Hugh Ross opened the circus yesterday he expressed the hope that "Nessie" would long remain in Loch Ness.

"Our pre-war offer for the legal capture of the monster still stands," Mr Mills told a representative of "The Press and Journal." "I think all this talk suggesting that the monster enjoys special protective rights should be dismissed as an unnecessary headache. Just imagine there being an Act of Parliament to protect a monster!"

Inverness-shire police headquarters staff were yesterday searching their archives for official direction on the subject. They did so at the request of the fiscal, who at the time knew nothing, of the Bertram Mills offer.

Aberdeen Journal - Saturday 23 August 1947

"NESSIE" PLAYS TO GALLERY
Gathering of Forty Watch Her Sun-bathing

The Loch Ness monster had its biggest-ever "reception committee" watching it as it sunned itself on the surface near Temple Pier for a full half-hour yesterday.

"Nessie" was not in a mood for dashing up the loch at speed and causing a flurry in the calm water. Instead, she cruised slowly along with two of her humps exposed to the sun.

Eighteen-year-old John M. Martin, St Margaret's, Midmills, Inverness, who was cycling to Drumnadrochit, came upon a car party at the roadside around 12.30 p.m., when he was about two miles from Temple Pier.

The gathering were watching a "big, black object," which was then about three-quarters of a mile out on the loch.

When Martin returned to the scene after having gone to Drumnadrochit to transact business, he found that the number of spectators watching the monster had increased to forty.

He described it as having two very large humps, but no head was visible and there was no backwash.

It eventually turned slowly towards the Inverness end of the loch.

A confirmed sceptic until yesterday, Martin added, "I used to scoff at the Loch Ness monster, but now I am convinced it is really there."

Dundee Evening Telegraph - Tuesday 15 June 1948

Sceptical Englishman Claims View Of Nessie

The best view for years of the Loch Ness monster was obtained by George Dines, Crumlin, Weymouth, who described himself as a "sceptical Englishman."

He was on holiday with his wife at Foyers Hotel, situated high above the centre of the loch and 20 miles from Inverness.

Mr Dines told a reporter- "I saw something large disporting itself in Foyers Bay. I immediately called people from the hotel, and six came.

"The object the loch was about 200 yards out in the bay, and it made straight across in the direction of the factory works. There was absolutely no doubt about it being something big. We didn't see the whole length of it at once. The head part came up and the back part came up later 20 or 30 feet away. It was a most amazing sight.

"The head part was huge, with ripples of water extending out from it on either side.

"The loch was absolutely flat calm. We had two sets of binoculars. The monster was travelling very slowly. It came up lazily, sipping along, and except [???] tremendous distrbance round the [???] there was no trail in the water [???] you would have in the wake of a boat. After travelling about 400 yards it passed from our sight.

Mrs Kenneth Grant of the hotel and another five persons verified the story.

About three weeks ago the monster was seen by Mr Pearson, Abriachan.

Dundee Courier - Saturday 19 June 1948

Was It Nessie Or Not?

Five people motoring from Inverness to Fort-William have reported an unusual sight in Loch Ness, opposite Urquhart Castle, but owing to their distance from it they do not claim to have seen the "Monster."

Driver of the car was Mr Thomas Skinner, a well-known Inverness master baker. Accompanying him were his daughter, Mr John E. Clark, of Montrose, and his son, and Mrs Mackenzie, a holidaymaker from Dundee.

Mr Skinner said their attention was drawn to wild splashes far out in the loch, which was otherwise calm.

"We watched the splashes for 20 minutes," declared Mr Skinner, "and we saw a black object which eventually disappeared, leaving white foam on the surface. It was all very strange, but too far away for me to give an exact description."

Mr Clark said the object was moving, and the surface was greatly disturbed. He was convinced there was something "abnormal" in the loch.

Aberdeen Journal - Friday 16 July 1948

Monster Gains New Converts
15-Minute Cruise at Invermoriston

Latest report of an appearance by the Loch Ness monster comes from Invermoriston.

Mr Jack Macdonald, forestry worker, and some of his mates watched it cruise along the surface of the water for fifteen minutes.

Mr Macdonald said that he and his workmates noticed a strange-looking object break the calm surface of the loch just off Altsaigh Youth Hostel. It moved slowly along. then turned shore-wards and plunged out of sight.

Mr Macdonald, who until then had been dubious of the monster's existence, is now quite certain that the loch holds an uncommon creature, "neither whale, seal, porpoise nor giant eel as has often been suggested by people who have never seen it for themselves."

On this occasion the monster was described as resembling an upturned boat.

Aberdeen Journal - Saturday 31 July 1948

Enter Maggie, the Morar Monster

Nine people went out in a motor boat on Loch Morar, Inverness-shire, Scotland's deepest loch, yesterday - and saw a monster. They called it Maggie.

Maggie wasn't a porpoise. She wasn't a salmon. She was like nothing any them had seen before.

She had five humps. She was dark in colour, and she reared up before them about 400 yards away.

Frank Fleet, Liverpool, saw her first. Then Mr James Doig, Glasgow, had a look through field glasses. So did the local boatman, Mr John Gillies.

Mrs Doig came back to Morar Hotel and said: "It's no fairy tale. Wouldn't have believed it unless I had seen it. It was the strangest thing I have ever clapped eyes on."

Maggie appeared for four minutes then disappeared. She was about 20 feet long, but neither her head nor tail was visible as she played about the surface of the loch.

Some local people were wondering whether in fact it was the Loch monster under a different name, because there is an old legend that under the loch runs a subterranean passage linking Morar with Loch Ness.

Dundee Courier - Saturday 31 July 1948

NESSIE HAS RIVAL IN LOCH MORAR MONSTER

A monster has appeared in the deepest inland loch in Scotland - Loch Morar, West Inverness-shire.

It was seen yesterday by a party of nine who were out cruising in a motor boat.

Mr John Gillies, 36 year-old boatman, said his attention was drawn by one of the passengers, Frank Fleet, of Widnes, to an unusual object moving through the water over a ½ of a mile away.

"I put the binoculars on to it," said Gillies. "It appeared to be about 20 feet long, and had five prominent humps. Neither head nor tail was visible.

"It wasn't travelling fast, about five knots, I would say, and remained several minutes on the surface.

"I have been familiar with this loch for 24 years, and I have never seen anything like it."

Mr Frank Fleet described it as a strange looking sight. "The loch was calm as a mill pond," he said, "and we watched the monster for three or four minutes before it finally disappeared.

"Mr James Doig, Croftfoot, Glasgow, another of the party, said he had always been inclined to laugh at monster stories, but added, "I am not laughing now."

Several times this summer the Loch Ness monster has been seen, especially near the Foyers area.

Dundee Courier - Saturday 31 July 1948

ANOTHER LOCH MYSTERY

Has "Nessie" a rival? At least Loch Ness has no longer a monopoly of monster mystery.

The report of a motor-boat party of nine who yesterday saw in Loch Morar a 20-foot creature disporting itself is not to be dismissed lightly. The watchers were at a quarter-mile range, but had binoculars to aid them, and a boatman with 24 years' experience of the loch as fellow-witness.

It is not enough for the sceptics to smile at the account of five humps as a mere copying of the Loch Ness legend. Nor does the optical illusion theory, attributed to freak wind-ripples on the surface, fit the Loch Morar phenomenon, for the water yesterday was mirror-calm. And there was no emulation of Nessie's turn of speed

The Morar apparition should set the zoologists a new problem, for this is an inland loch. A pity if the mystery is turned off with a knowing comment on the opening of the August holiday season.

Dundee Courier - Friday 24 December 1948

MOTORISTS SEE LOCH MONSTER

Mrs Ellice, wife of Mr Russell Ellice, of Glengarry, a well-known Inverness-shire family, said she and her two children had a wonderful view of the Loch Ness monster yesterday.

They were motoring towards Inverness. When approaching Brackla, several miles east of Urquhart Castle, they saw a motor lorry drawn up. The driver was pointing excitedly towards the loch.

Mrs Ellice stopped the car, and there, less than 160 yards offshore, the monster was bobbing up and down. The loch was calm as a millpond.

Mrs Ellice said its head reminded her somewhat of a seal's, but this was a really huge creature.

"We are all thrilled," she added, "more especially as I had never believed in the monster's existence."

Mrs Ellice and her children, along with the driver, watched the monster for about ten minutes. When they continued their journey it was still moving about on the surface.

Aberdeen Journal - Friday 24 December 1948

Loch Ness Monster Up for Christmas Ten-minute Display Before Motorists

The Loch Ness monster, after a long period of inactivity, gave a ten-minute display yesterday before a party of motorists proceeding to Inverness.

Included in the party were Mrs Ellice, wife of Mr Russell Ellice, Glengarry, and her two children.

When approaching Brackla, several miles east of Urquhart Castle, they were signalled to stop by the driver of a motor lorry who was pointing towards the loch.

Mrs Ellice stopped immediately and there, less than 150 yards offshore, the monster was disporting itself.

The head was well above the surface and there was a considerable commotion in the water caused by the huge body.

The loch was as calm as a millpond and visibility excellent.

Mrs Ellice told a reporter of "The Press and Journal" that it reminded her of a seal although there was no comparison as to size. It was a really huge creature and quite unlike anything she had ever seen before.

Adelaide News (Australia) - Tuesday 11 January 1949

Former S.A. man saw "monster" of Loch Ness

The Loch Ness monster has been reported again, which prompts a man well known in Adelaide - the Rev. Gordon Powell, who for several years was in charge of Port Adelaide Presbyterian Church - to tell how he saw the "monster."

"It has been suggested that those who claim to have seen the monster are more in need of a psychiatrist than a zoologist," says Mr. Powell. "If so, I am a serious case."

This is the story told by Mr. Powell, who is now at Collins Street Independent Church, Melbourne:-

"I was on a camping tour with another Australian and a Scot. The three of us were doing a post-graduate course in theology at Glasgow University.

"We had pitched our tent beside the picturesque Urquhart Castle, half-way down the loch. The day was June 21, 1936.

At 5.30 on that Sunday afternoon I was sitting on the hillside overlooking the centre. of the loch, and to the left the little inlet running into the village of Drumnadrochit.

"As it was the longest day of the year, there was plenty of light, nightfall coming at about 10.30 in that part of Scotland. It was unusually bright, and the first time I had felt uncomfortably hot in Britain.

"My two friends were away in the car, and I was writing a letter at the time. I happened to look up - when the monster suddenly appeared... I nearly ran the pencil through the paper.

"To my amazement, I saw three, and sometimes four, humps moving rapidly through the water... as though they were the coils of a huge sea-serpent.

"I hastily seized my camera, but as the range was about 200 yards the photograph registered only the white wake left in the water. The monster dived at a point said to be 700 ft. deep.

"Several people reported to the press having seen what I saw at the same time and place."

After 12 years Mr. Powell remains steadfast in his belief. He advances the theory that, as similar monsters are known to have existed long ago, there is a possibility of an odd one surviving in a lake now cut off from the sea with which it was once connected.

There it would be safe from its natural enemies, and only seen at rare intervals because its natural habitat would be the extreme depth of Loch Ness.

His description is typical of almost all reports of the strange animal - the seal-like head, the serpentine neck and the great size. These are important points, for they fit explanations put forward by zoologists.

Mr. Powell says that, with the development of radar during the war and the remarkably efficient submarine detecting devices used by whalers, it should not be long before the movements of the monster can be tracked so it can be photographed at close range and perhaps captured.

Dundee Courier - Tuesday 06 September 1949

Ex-Policeman Sees The Monster

Mr George Cameron, warden of the Scottish Youth Hostel at Alltsaigh, near Invermoriston, has seen the Loch Ness monster.

This summer it has made only a few appearances, the last known being in June.

Mr Cameron, who retired last May after 30 years with Inverness County Police, said he noticed the monster break the loch's calm surface about 800 yards out. It cruised along showing the head and a large hump like an upturned boat.

After a minute and a half it plunged out of sight, throwing up a huge wash.

"I called, and my assistant warden, Colin Cameron, Main Road, Elgin came at once. The monster reappeared shortly afterwards, and meanwhile I got out my binoculars and clearly saw three humps.

"Each was ten feet long and fully ten feet separated them. It moved off in the direction of Fort-Augustus at 30 miles an hour. Its skin was dark grey and crinkly, like an elephant's.

Previously Mr Cameron was sceptical of the monster's existence, but now he is fully convinced, and thinks some scientific body should investigate.

Aberdeen Journal - Tuesday 06 September 1949

Monster Performs for Former Policeman
'Humps Ten Feet Long - Speed 30 m.p.h.'

Following a period of three months' inactivity, the. Loch Ness monster has been seen again - this time by a man who previously did not believe in its existence.

He is Mr George Cameron, who has been warden of the Scottish Youth Hostel at Altsaigh, Invermoriston, since retiring from Inverness County Constabulary last May after thirty years' service.

In an interview, Mr Cameron stated that his attention was attracted to the Loch by the appearance of something breaking the calm surface, some eight hundred yards out.

A head and one hump, like an upturned boat, came into view, and the monster cruised about for a minute and a half, then dived, leaving a tremendous swirl.

Mr Cameron shouted to his wife and to the assistant warden. Mr Colin Cameron (no relative), 7 Mayne Road, Elgin, but Mrs Cameron did not hear him.

Both Saw It

The assistant warden joined him and, shortly afterwards they both saw the monster surface again, this time showing three humps.

"These humps," said Mr Cameron, "were ten feet long and two feet high, and there was at least ten feet between each hump, which gives a total length of fifty feet. That would not be all, as the head and tail were still submerged."

But what impressed Mr Cameron most was the speed at which the monster began to travel before it finally vanished some minutes later. This he estimated to be 30 m.p.h.

On its second appearance, Mr Cameron had the monster under observation through powerful binoculars.

He clearly saw that its skin appeared rough and was of a grey colour, very like an elephant's.

It is now over sixty years since the monster struck the headlines in the Press, and Mr Cameron thinks the time has come for the matter to be fully investigated by some competent authority.

1950s

Dundee Courier - Saturday 29 April 1950

Nessie Makes 1950 Debut

The Loch Ness monster has made a reappearance after a long spell.

Lady Maud Baillie, who is staying near Ballindalloch Lodge, was accompanied on a tour of the loch side by her two granddaughters and her cousin, Lady Spring-Rice.

While Lady Maud was pointing out the ancient Glen Urquhart Castle the little girl asked if a black object in the loch was a rock.

The loch was calm, and the object began to move, and rushed through the water at high speed. It left a long white wash.

The party left the car and made for the side of the loch to get a closer view, but the object disappeared.

The part of the loch where the party saw the monster is the spot where it has been seen previously during spring months.

Aberdeen Journal - Tuesday 09 May 1950

Glimpse of 'Nessie's' Three Humps

The first real day of summer in the Highlands yesterday brought Nessie to the surface of Loch Ness in the forenoon.

For almost two minutes she swam about the loch being seen by a party of workmen who were carrying out road repairs midway between Inverness and Drumnadrochit.

During this swim the monster was seen also by Mr Callum Morrison, a contractor, of Brown Street, Inverness, and Mr Andrew Russell, a van driver, Pumpgate Street, Inverness.

Mr Russell told reporter of "The Press and Journal" that he first saw the monster about thirty or forty yards from the shore, and although the head was hidden under the water, three humps were clearly visible.

"It created a tremendous wash and waves almost a foot high broke on the shore," he said.

Dundee Courier - Wednesday 21 June 1950

A Spot...
Two Coils...
It's Nessie

Three people who visited Foyers, Inverness-shire, report having seen the Loch Ness monster, and have given a vivid description of the incident.

The witnesses are Mr S. Hunter Gordon, managing director of Resistance Welders, Inverness and London, who was accompanied by Mr C. E. Dunton, of London Transport, and Mr Dunton's son.

The loch was calm and visibility was excellent when Mr Dunton's son saw a dark object. He thought it was a rock, but when it moved he called his father, who joined him.

They saw two long coils, and watched the object through a telescope. As one of the coils disappeared they called on Mr Gordon, who was in time to see the remaining coil disappear.

"I had no doubt that it was the monster," said Mr Gordon, "as I have had the pleasure along with another well-known Inverness citizen of having seen the monster in 1939."

Aberdeen Journal - Saturday 22 July 1950

'Nessie' Puts on Show for Visitors

An Inverness taxi-driver and four holidaymakers yesterday saw the Loch Ness monster disporting itself for a short time near Drumnadrochit Bay.

The taximan, Mr Finlay Macrae, 3 Ness-side. was driving his four passengers along the west side of Loch Ness when "Nessie" was spotted. He stopped the car, and all went out for a better view.

Mr Macrae described the monster as having a head like a Cheviot sheep without ears, while the underside was yellowish grey.

"I have been fishing the loch for about twenty years," he added, "but without having seen the monster before."

Aberdeen Journal - Saturday 29 July 1950

'Monster' With a Head 2ft. Wide

A "Loch Ness monster" has appeared in the sea off Margate. Mr J. Handley, of Wembley, who is on holiday, declares he saw it yesterday. "It had ears like a horse," he said. "I saw only its head, but that was over 2ft. wide."

Aberdeen Journal - Monday 31 July 1950

Eyes on Loch Ness

From to-morrow onwards for a month earnest young eyes will be scanning Loch Ness, looking for signs of the monster. One hundred and fifty senior Boy Scouts from various parts of Britain will watch the loch with binoculars and cameras from dawn to dusk, in the hope of settling once and for all if there is, or is not, a mysterious denizen of the deeps.

Loch Ness is over twenty-two miles long, one mile broad on an average, and from 240 to 780 feet deep, so that the monster has plenty of cover.

One does not know whether to wish the Scouts luck or not. At least they will be content with proving its existence, unlike some previous hunters who proposed to capture or murder the beast (if there is one).

But if the Scouts identify it, the mystery will be gone; and in our workaday world a little bit of innocent mystery is a refreshment to the imagination. On the other hand, if they fail, that will not show the monster is not there, and the holiday-makers by the loch can go on speculating and watching.

Sunday Post - Sunday 13 August 1950

He Saw The Tail Of The Loch Ness Monster!

On July 22, my family and I were cycling alongside Loch Ness, when my attention was attracted to an unusual pattern on the water about a hundred yards off-shore.

The creature making the pattern changed course and came in our direction. As it came nearer, we could see two fin-like objects about six feet apart and opposite each other.

It came to within about twenty yards of the shore and suddenly turned. As it did so, we could see part of a black tail-like object churning the water. It made out across the loch.

Hoping the creature would surface, we grabbed our bikes and dashed down the road. But when it was about a hundred yards away it turned and, travelling at terrific speed for some yards, the two fins disappeared under the surface.

I realise my tale will be ridiculed many quarters. But I am convinced that it's only a matter of time before someone gets a photograph that will remove all doubt about the presence of some creature in the waters of Loch Ness. - A. K. Wright, 634 Boydstone Road, Carnwadric. Glasgow.

Aberdeen Journal - Wednesday 30 August 1950

Loch Ness Monster Seen by Busload of Tourists

A party of English and Scottish tourists on bus tour from the Richmond Hotel, Strathpeffer, to Fort-Augustus, yesterday had a clear view of the Loch Ness monster for fifteen minutes.

First to see the monster was the driver of the bus, Mr David Douglas, Edinburgh, who has done the tour many times during the past three years and has always been sceptical about there being anything unusual in the loch.

He is now completely convinced that there is a monster. He had a "perfectly clear view" of it yesterday.

10 m.p.h.

One of the passengers, Mr James Murray, Lismore Crescent, Edinburgh, said they were passing Castle Urquhart, beyond Drumnadrochit, on the way to Fort-Augustus, when they saw what appeared to be an "enlarged duck's head" travelling in the direction or Castle Urquhart at a speed of about ten miles an hour.

The monster was putting up a strong wash behind it and making a great disturbance in the water, caused, it seemed, by the wriggle of its tail.

From head to tail he estimated it to be 30ft. long, but they saw no humps.

They stopped the bus and the passengers watched the monster for about fifteen minutes, having a real close-up of the monster's activities.

It was still swimming strongly when they left for Fort-Augustus.

There was great excitement among all members of the party.

'Now Convinced'

The loch was like a mirror and hills behind were reflected in the water.

Another passenger, Miss Mary Maresova, Cheltenham, said that the head looked like a floating mine.

Another, Mr A. S. Blundell, Forest Hill, London, said: "The monster came out from the side of the loch, took a sharp turn right, and went off up the loch. I did not believe the story before, but I am now convinced of the truth of the Loch Ness monster. I clearly saw its tail flapping about 30ft. from its head.

"We were surprised, as we stood on the shores watching it, when another coach passed us but did not stop. The head was about 2ft. in size, black in colour, and the Monster had a white breast."

When the party left Strathpeffer for their run down the loch yesterday, the driver of another bus called to them that they were sure see the monster that day. They did!

Dundee Courier - Wednesday 30 August 1950

TOURISTS SAW THE MONSTER

A party of excited coach tourists returned to their headquarters at Strathpeffer last night with the claim that for 15 minutes yesterday they had watched the Loch Ness Monster - some said they had taken pictures of it.

First to see the monster was the driver of the bus, Mr David Douglas, Edinburgh. He has done the run many times during the past three years, and has always been sceptical about the monster. He is now convinced.

One of the passengers, Mr James Murray. Lismore Crescent, Edinburgh, said they had just passed Castle Urquhart when the driver drew their attention to a ripple on the loch about three-quarters of a mile away.

The bus was stopped, and the fifteen members of the party - men and women from Scotland and England, - saw, as Mr Murray described it, "something like an enlarged duck's head travelling in the direction of Castle Urquhart and putting up a strong wash 30 feet behind it.

"We watched it for 15 minutes, when it must have travelled at least a couple of miles. We had to go on because we were on a scheduled tour. It was still swimming fast when we set off. There was great excitement in the party. The loch was like a mirror, with the hills behind reflected in it. It was along this reflection that the monster was swimming."

LIKE FLOATING MINE

Another passenger, Miss Mary Maresova, of Cheltenham, said the head looked to her at first like a floating mine.

Mr A. S. Blundell, of Forest Hill, London, said, "The monster came out from the other side of the loch, swam towards us then took a sharp turn right and swam strongly up the loch parallel to the road.

"I never believed the monster story, but now I am fully convinced. We clearly saw the tail flapping about 30 feet from the head. The head was about two feet long, black in colour with a white breast. It was going very fast - I should say about 10 miles an hour."

Miss Higgs, of Brian Road, Twickenham, Middlesex, said she gave her camera to Mr Murray, and he focussed on the head, which he could see well out of the water. He estimated its speed at 15 to 20 miles an hour.

Others in the party who saw the monster were Miss Mary Entwistle, Kew Road, Richmond, Surrey; Miss Margo Mellor, Sheen Park, Richmond; and Mrs James Murray, Edinburgh.

Dundee Courier - Saturday 30 June 1951

Loch Ness monster appears again

Two appearances by the Loch Ness monster on successive evenings were recorded in Inverness yesterday.

On Thursday evening a fishing gillie, Robert Burrill, a fellow employee, Roderick McLean, and a London chauffeur were fishing in the vicinity of Urquhart Castle when Burrill saw what he thought to be a log on the surface of the loch 200 yards ahead of the boat and 30 yards from the shore.

"When we were 70 yards from it," said Burrill, "it moved off at a terrific speed into the centre of the loch and then submerged."

On the previous evening an army officer from Fort George, out fishing from the other side of the loch, saw it speeding up the loch, which was calm at the time.

Aberdeen Evening Express - Tuesday 11 September 1951

Nessie Convinces Sceptic

The Loch Ness monster was seen to-day about tour miles west of Bona Ferry by 81-year-old crofter Duncan Chisholm, Balloan, Caplich; two 13-year-old boys, Jacky Ross and Melvyn Waller; and Miss J. Macdonald, Abriachan.

Mr Chisholm, who has lived on the lochside all his life, and did not believe in the monster, said that he was now convinced of its existence.

"The two boys drew my attention to what they described as a big fish in the water," he said, "and we all watched it for about five minutes."

Mr Chisholm said that the monster looked like a submarine in the water. Although the loch was calm, the monster created a terrific wash despite the fact that it was travelling at a slow speed.

Dundee Courier - Friday 29 February 1952

Three men say
They got a glimpse of Nessie

The Loch Ness monster has made its 1952 debut. It was seen yesterday evening by three Inverness men travelling home from Invergarry.

They are Mr David Macdonald, 18 Telford Gardens; Mr Murdoch Mackenzie, Craigton Avenue; and Mr Thomas Campbell.

Mr Macdonald stated that shortly after leaving Invergarry, Mr Campbell, who was driving the lorry, drew their attention to white foam on Loch Ness about 500 yards out from the shore.

They stopped and went to the bank, where they had a clear view of the monster speeding in the direction of Invergarry.

The loch was comparatively calm at the time, and they observed a wake of foam which was creating quite a wash on the shore of the loch.

"I saw three fair-sized black humps protruding out of the water," said Mr Macdonald. "We, quite excited, watched it go at considerable speed and then it submerged. The hump came into view once more for a moment then disappeared.

"The object was anything from 15 to 18 feet long, and I am convinced the monster definitely exists."

Aberdeen Evening Express - Friday 11 April 1952

Monster Time Is Here Again With Head, Neck And Three Humps

The Loch Ness Monster was seen this morning by a bus load of passengers and a few motorists.

They claim to have had a perfect view of it moving slowly in the Inverness direction. They were watching from the top of Croft Brae, near Dores, about ten miles from Inverness.

The bus driver, Mr John Macaskill (38), 6 Temple Crescent, Inverness, who said he used to "scoff and laugh" at the idea of a monster, is now convinced of its existence.

He told an "Evening Express" reporter to-day that when he saw the monster it was in the middle of the loch and its head, neck and three humps were clearly visible.

Two of the humps, he said, were prominent although the third was a little obscured. The bus passengers, he added, all went to one side of the bus and were overjoyed at what they had seen.

They watched the monster for about ten minutes before it slowly submerged, said Mr Macaskill.

Mr William Fraser, 19a Drummond Road, Inverness, clerk of works with Inverness County Council, also saw the monster. It was he who stopped the bus to tell the driver that "it was on show."

Miss Evelyn Maclennan, bus conductress, also had a "perfect view" of the monster about 10.45 a.m. when returning from Fort William to Inverness.

Dundee Courier - Tuesday 29 April 1952

Nessie again - doing 25 m.p.h.

The Loch Ness monster made its second reported appearance this year, when it was observed yesterday afternoon by two civil engineers from Inverness County Water Department, who were motoring from Fort-Augustus to Inverness.

They are Mr William MacDonald, 63 Balliseary Road, Inverness, and Mr Alistair MacLean, Golf View Hotel, Milburn Road, Inverness.

Mr MacDonald stated that three miles from Fort-Augustus they observed a terrific wash 160 yards out from the loch side, the water otherwise being quite calm at the time.

They saw a neck and head sticking three feet out of the water about eight inches in diameter, the head tapering to point like that of a snake.

They kept level with the object, which was creating a great wake, travelling at about 25 miles per hour. They had to stop the car when their view was obstructed by trees. By the time they got down to the lochside , the object had disappeared.

Dundee Courier - Friday 22 August 1952

Nessie camera-shy

The Loch Ness monster was reported to have been seen yesterday by an Inverness woman and her 13-year-old son.

She was Mrs H. Finlay, 3 Midmills Road, wife of an Inverness stationer.

The monster's latest appearance was at the east end of the loch, where Mrs Finlay and her son Harry were caravaning.

They heard the sound of splashing water, and on turning round saw the monster quite near the shore, but moving quickly away. Two parts of the creature's body - the familiar bumps - were visible above surface, but before Mrs Finlay could get her camera focused the monster had disappeared.

This was at noon, and children at Dores were reported to have seen it at 2 p.m.

Scene of the monster's latest appearance is several miles from the area likely to be selected by John Cobb for his forthcoming attempt on the world's speed-boat record.

Yorkshire Post and Leeds Intelligencer - Monday 12 July 1954

The Loch Ness monster again

For the first time this summer the Loch Ness Monster is reported to have been seen.

While boating on the loch at the weekend Miss Margaret MacDonald, 21-year-old hotel waitress, and Kenneth Mackintosh, 18-year-old farm worker, both of Lewiston, Invernesshire, saw the loch's surface disturbed near Urquhart. Then they saw what appeared to the Monster crossing the bay towards Temple Pier on the same side of the loch.

Miss MacDonald said that a head and three humps were visible above the surface, and these remained in view for about five minutes.

The Loch Ness Monster, reported more than 20 years ago, last made its appearance in December when five woodcutters stated they saw it in Urquhart Castle Bay.

Dundee Courier - Friday 23 July 1954

Woman tells of "Nessie's" appearance

A woman says she watched the Loch Ness monster for nearly ten minutes yesterday afternoon a short distance from Fort Augustus Abbey.

The woman, Miss Elizabeth Macgruer, Oich Cottage, Fort Augustus, said she saw the monster appear off the mouth of the River Oich.

A long thin neck and three humps came in sight, and the monster moved quickly across the loch towards Borlum Bay.

Aberdeen Evening Express - Saturday 14 August 1954

100 People Saw Nessie Yesterday

Nessie - the Loch Ness monster - now really exists for 100 people who saw her surface near Castle Urquhart yesterday.

Three bus loads, more than a dozen motorists, and several local people saw a disturbance in the water, and then a form of dark substance which spread over the water like oil.

First to spot Nessie was Ewan Fraser (70), former custodian of the castle, who lives nearby.

"The water was quite calm when I noticed that a flock of wild duck, which had been swimming peacefully, suddenly scatter and fly off," he said.

Dark Deposit

"Almost at once I saw two wakes moving out from the shore. The next thing I saw was a dark deposit, rather like oil, which spread out in two lines after the wakes had faded out."

Another man, Donald Maclean (31), builder, 33 Lovat Road, Inverness, claimed to have seen Nessie's hump.

He was travelling to work with another man and they had been discussing the phenomenon. Sceptically Mr MacLean had said she was a basking shark.

"On seeing what I saw, however, I changed mind," he said afterwards. "It was definitely no basking shark. I borrowed a telescope from a Norwegian camper and clearly saw a hump slicking about two feet out of the water.

"The hump was between the two wakes and appeared to be white, but I attribute this to the action of the sunlight on its wet surface.

"This was no hoax," he added, "but I wish someone had managed to get a sample of that deposit. It would have been the first concrete evidence of the monster's existence."

Dundee Courier - Tuesday 17 August 1954

Monster gives a display for Mr McMillan

Mr Peter McMillan, head gamekeeper on the Glenmoriston estate, saw the Loch Ness monster at the week-end.

He watched it for several minutes, and said what impressed him most was the monster's size, speed, and strength.

Mr McMillan estimated the total length of the two humps at 35 feet. Neither the head nor neck was visible.

"The humps, which were brown in colour and looked tough, reminded me of the skin of an elephant and in form were like upturned boats.

"After covering a mile on the surface, the monster submerged in the direction of Fort Augustus."

Dundee Courier - Saturday 04 December 1954

Nessie on the screen

The Loch Ness monster has been seen again.

She appeared this time on the echo-sounding screen of the Peterhead fishing vessel The Rival, which was passing through the Loch bound for the West Coast fishing grounds.

"We were a short distance east of Urquhart Castle when this strange image showed up on the screen. The object was 90 fathoms below the surface," said Mr Peter Anderson, the mate, when a "Courier" reporter went on board.

The image was parallel with the ship's keel, and covered about 1¼ inches on the screen. It showed a round head, a curving, tapering tail, and what appeared to be four legs stretching from the body.

Mr Anderson estimated the length at 50 feet.

"We were steaming slowly at the time and the instrument took about five minutes to record the image."

Aberdeen Evening Express - Saturday 04 December 1954

Nessie Seen 90 Fathoms Down

Nessie, the Loch Ness monster, may or may not appear on TV, but she has just appeared the screen of a herring drifter's echo sounder.

This was revealed last night by Mr Peter Anderson, mate of the Peterhead drifter Rival, who said that while the Rival was passing through the loch on her way to the west coast, a strange image showed up on the screen, registered at about ninety fathoms below the surface.

A Round Head

The image, which was parallel with the ship's keel, covered about one and a quarter inches on the screen, and showed a round head and a curving, tapering tail, and what appeared to be four legs projecting from the underside of the body.

Mr Anderson estimated the length of the body at fifty feet. He said the drifter was steaming slowly at the time, and the instrument took about five minutes to record the image of the monster.

The incident occurred while the vessel was short distance east of Castle Urquhart.

Also Available

LOCH NESS:
From Out Of The Depths
Original Newspaper Accounts of the Rise
of the Loch Ness Monster, 1933-1934

In 1933 "Nessie" erupted into the public consciousness with a deluge of sightings of "something" in the waters of the 22 mile long and 700 foot deep Scottish loch. Since then the Loch Ness Monster has captured the public imagination more than any other cryptid creature.

Gathered in this book are the original newspaper accounts from the years 1933 and 1934, when "Nessie Fever" was at its height. Not just sightings, but plans for monster hunts and government responses to the appearance of this unknown creature are presented here.

Whatever your stance on the existence of the Loch Ness Monster, these accounts provide a fascinating insight into the happenings and opinions that swirled around Loch Ness in the early part of the 20th Century.

Available in paperback and for Kindle from Amazon.com

Also Available

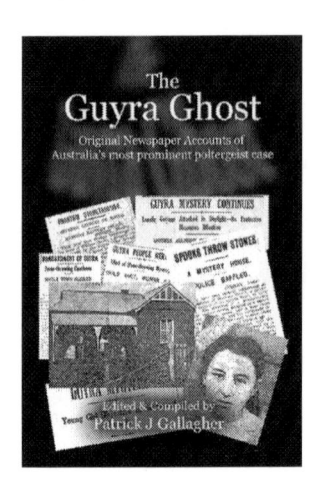

The Guyra Ghost
Original Newspaper Accounts of Australia's Most Prominent Poltergeist Case

APRIL, 1921 – GUYRA, NSW. For over a month in 1921, the tiny town of Guyra in northern NSW was the focus of national attention as events unfolded that would form the basis of Australia's most prominent poltergeist case, as the home of the Bowen family was bombarded by stones from nowhere, and the walls were pounded on by unseen hands.

Here, for the first time, is a collection of all the available newspaper articles that were published regarding the incident at the time. From this evidence you may draw your own conclusions. Hoax? Or a true case of paranormal phenomena...?

Available in paperback and for Kindle from Amazon.com

Also Available

THE TANTANOOLA TIGER
And Other Australian Big Cat Sightings

Original Early Newspaper Accounts of Anomalous and Mysterious Big Cat Sightings in the Australian Bush

At the end of the 19th Century, and even into the early 20th Century, large areas of eastern Australia were still in a state that could be regarded as "wilderness". From these fringes came reports concerning creatures that would be somewhat mundane were it not for the out-of-place nature of their appearances.

Tigers and lions.

Whether it was a case of mistaken identity, people seeing thylacines (Tasmanian Tigers), or that people had not yet come to terms with how large feral cats could become in the wild, there were many sightings of *something* prowling the Australian bush.

Available in paperback and for Kindle from Amazon.com

Printed in Great Britain
by Amazon